EMPOWER.
PROMOTE.
LAUNCH.

[REPEAT]

Create a culture
of Generational Leadership
using four CORE strategies

JEREMY GRAVES

Contents

FOREWORD I

INTRODUCTION: BECOMING A LEGACY MAKER XI

LESSONS FROM THE TRADITIONALISTS 1

THE BABY BOOMER MESSAGE 11

GENERATION X: THE "WHO CARES" GENERATION 21

THE MILLENNIAL "GENERATION ME" MYTH 33

READY OR NOT, HERE COMES GENERATION Z 47

GETTING TO THE CORE 57

COLLABORATION IN THE 21ST CENTURY WORKFORCE 63

CLEARING MUDDY OBJECTIVES 69

RAISING UP LEADERS UPON LEADERS 79

EMPOWERING YOUR TEAM 97

COMMITTING TO THE PROCESS 111

CONCLUSION: ARE YOU A LEGACY MAKER? 119

ACKNOWLEDGMENTS 123

REFERENCES 125

FOREWORD

My earliest example of organizational leadership was my dad. He was a visionary entrepreneur who was collaborative and always respectful toward his employees. He was never fixated on creating wealth. Instead, he was an entrepreneur because he enjoyed living his values through his work. He encouraged me as a teenager to innovate and together we developed new solutions to a problem at General Motors that saved tens of thousands of dollars and made me feel like I was making a positive difference.

Later, I was given a copy of Peter Drucker's, "The Effective Executive" and I learned that there was something special about being a leader, beyond authority, status or pay. I began to realize that leading is a significant way to serve others and help them gain self-esteem. As a leader, it was possible to inspire someone else to make larger commitments to their own growth and future, all while building a successful business.

Today, forty-five years later, I'm more fascinated by the topic of leadership than ever. I have come to believe that we are all leaders in one way or another because we all have opportunities to be influencers. For me, this opportunity to influence others is one of the great privileges of life. As I begin to envision the end of my career as a leadership coach, I'm looking for others who will carry the baton and serve with the same passion that has served me so well.

Jeremy Graves is one of those people. His passion for serving others gives me great encouragement for the future. His insights about connecting with people across generations is helpful, no matter what your age or experience. The guidance for developing others through his CORE philosophy captures the fundamental opportunities we have as leaders to change the lives of employees, teams, organizations, and ultimately, the world we all live in.

The leadership journey is far different today from when I started my own adventure in the late 60s. Many trends of the 21st century are challenging assumptions and practices that, though they may have been helpful in the past, will sabotage our success going forward. These are times when we all need to embrace humility and learn new skills to be part of tomorrow's success.

This book offers fresh thinking to guide your path forward. I encourage you to read it carefully. Take notes of your own thoughts as you proceed. Allow yourself to think differently. Create an action plan and commit to follow through. If you are so inclined, reach out to Jeremy for help. There is treasure here, waiting for those who will take advantage of Jeremy's insights.

Ron Price
CEO Price Associates
April 2018

had just finished speaking at a sales conference on attracting millennial clients when a gentleman approached me in his late 70's. As he approached, he reached out his hand to shake mine with a genuine smile on his face. "Well done young lady! It certainly is impressive what you've been able to do at such a young age." I began to thank him for such an earnest compliment when he continued, "Especially because you're a woman too!"

When I tell this story to conferences or groups of executives I work with, they usually lean in, expectantly waiting for me to share exactly how I set this old man straight. Sure, I could have been incredibly offended with just how out of touch this man appeared. If I had stormed off in a rage or told him what I thought of him and his generation, you would understand.

But I didn't.

I actually laughed and simply explained that I don't think about being young or being a woman when I work with leaders. I then thanked him and others like him who have mentored my generation along the way so we can start companies and write books and not have to think about our gender, age or race. This is not because I am a saintly person or have no emotions—if you saw me when there's a slow Internet connection and I'm trying to send an email for the fourth time, you would believe me. I was able to respond with perspective because I understood his generation's view on leadership. You see, in his generation, it was rare to see someone young on the stage—and nearly unheard of to see a young woman speaking in front of 500 businessmen.

As a millennial author and speaker, I have spoken on stages around the world and worked with presidential candidates, Fortune 500 CEOs and military generals. Although I may notice that I am the youngest and usually the only woman in the room, I never think too much about it.

Fifty years ago, it was extremely rare that a young woman was elevated as an expert. But what is normal for one generation does not mean it is permissible for the next. Brilliant whiz kids are starting multi-billion dollar companies in their dorm rooms, strong and strategic women are rising to the top of the corporate ladder, and millions of other amazing moments are changing the social norms that confined us to our labels. We still have work to do to bring parity for many within the workplace, but that shouldn't belittle the amazing progress we have seen in the last century.

What I have done in my young life has little to do with me and everything to do with the subject of the book in your hands. Legacy is a powerful concept that inspires, daunts and motivates each of us. Whether we vocalize it or not, leaders of all ages desire to have an impact on the world. Some may call it significance. Others consider it purpose. And still there are those that would simply admit they want to be remembered for doing something good.

I often tell audiences that millennial don't need older generations for information. They have the Internet for that. What millennial really need other generations for is the interpretation and application of that information. In this book, you will discover not only why great leaders are intentional about legacy. You will gain a clearer understanding of how to apply these principles—the CORE Team Leadership Model—within your own sphere of significance.

Yes, I am a millennial.

I was actually going to begin this foreword with the statement that I was a millennial, but I didn't. I began with a story of how one generation can accidentally offend another generation. Age discrimination is often not intentional but a natural reflection of your experience with individuals within that generation. Age discrimination is also not just the old discriminating against the young—there are plenty of millennial who have negative views of those older than themselves.

If the only thing you knew about me was my age, you may not take this seriously. You may question my legitimacy or even consider what you could learn from someone so young. Or perhaps you would have been interested to hear what a millennial has to say on legacy and leadership.

As someone who has conducted research on my generation for over 11 years and written four books on millennial motivation, I have experienced the power and the problems caused when generations work together. I have seen how stereotypes are easily placed on others because of their station or status or age or color. I have also seen what can happen when we start to think of others as individuals and not project our own expectations or experience upon them. The biggest mistake I see leaders make every day— from four-star military generals to main street shop owners—

is projecting their own experience on the next generation.

As one of my own mentors explained, "It is ignorant and arrogant to assume that the next generation should see the same world you see." As you will soon discover from this book, leadership is not just about how you lead. It is also about who you lead.

This book is a powerful step-by-step tool guiding you into what it means to create a culture and a movement powered by legacy. I encourage you to use it with your team, your community and your family to identify opportunities to grow your own legacy.

The second biggest mistake leaders make is postponing their legacy discussions until it's too late. Legacy talks somehow turn into a conversation around funeral arrangements and who gets what when you die. But that is not what legacy truly is. There are three principles of legacy to pursue with passion as you dive into this important book

Legacy is a choice.

No, legacy does not just happen. Legacy is both the most natural and the most unnatural occurrence in human interaction. For millennia, our existence depended on one generation passing their knowledge and wisdom onto the next generation. From cooking to hunting to child rearing, the human experience has expanded as we shared what we have learned with one another. This may not seem profound. Parents are hardwired to help their children prevent pain and pursue a better life than they once had.

However, this concept seems to have been lost in the modern workplace. Rather than helping those who are younger avoid mistakes, today's managers and leaders often want it to be harder for the next group of employees. As Jeremy explains in this book, legacy makers prioritize setting a vision, inspiring collaboration and empowering others. Legacy is an intentional act of passing the insight of one generation to the next. It is not an automatic transition, but takes patience, practice and a process.

Legacy has nothing to do with age.

Your legacy begins now. Whether you are 22, 62 or 102, you have a legacy. John Maxwell once defined leadership as influence—plain and simple. With that definition, it is hard to argue that everyone is not a leader.

The impact you have on others happens most often without you knowing it. Think back to the last encounter you had with someone that left an impression on you. It could have been with a stranger, a family member or a colleague. But there was something in the exchange that left you reflecting on what they said or did.

If you picked up this book and only think it's for leaders looking at retirement, think again. Jeremy has designed this book to be applicable to leaders of all ages seeking genuine influence and impact. After all, the individuals with the greatest legacies tend to start the earliest.

Legacy is both positive and negative.

What do you think of when you hear the word *legacy*? Is it a building, a movement, a child? Or is it something else entirely? Whatever is pictured in your mind at this moment is probably something positive.

However, legacies can be both positive and negative. A legacy can be a $2 billion fortune for your children to invest in philanthropic causes; but it could also be the hurt, neglect and regret your children now harbor towards you.

A legacy can be a debt-free international firm employing 10,000 employees; but it could also be a toxic dog-eat-dog culture where no one is quite sure if they're going to stick around.

My hope is that as you read through this book, you take the concepts to heart. In all of my work with top companies and international leaders, I have yet to see such a clear equation for legacy and influence. Jeremy has developed a stellar resource for you to use with your team, your family and your community.

It is an insightful analysis of how our generations impact our leadership style, and how you can best lead those who are different than you. It is a formula for determining how you and your company can develop and execute a vision that lasts.

You will discover more about yourself than you may expect to—or perhaps it is the pursuit of self-development that caused you to pick up this book.

No matter your motivation, I'm glad you are here.

On behalf of a generation in need of your wisdom, I want to say thank you. You are already showing a level of intentional leadership most never pursue. It is now up to you to use it.

Gabrielle Bosché
President of The Millennial Solution,
Bestselling Author, International Speaker

INTRODUCTION:
BECOMING A LEGACY MAKER

*"All good men and women must take responsibility to create legacies that
will take the next generation to a level we could only imagine."*
—Jim Rohn

Today is Mike's 65th birthday. Like any other day he rolls out of bed, grabs the newspaper and his cup of coffee, and settles in for his morning routine of catching up on the world and thinking through his day. As he scans the front page of the newspaper, his mind cannot shake a feeling of uncertainty. Mike is the CEO of Pure Energy. Pure Energy is facing some difficult times no thanks to the story on page three of today's newspaper headlining the cost of energy versus the benefits of going green. Mike has been watching this shift for the past several years in the energy sector and has even led his company through strategic planning that has pivoted his company to a place of prosperity. Mike has lived through uncertain times before, but this time it just seems different somehow.

As Mike reflects on his birthday and his future retirement, he begins to think about what kind of legacy he is leaving behind. He has seen leaders who get near the age of retirement and simply coast until their retirement party, shake a few hands, and then slowly fade away as the company moves forward without them at the helm. Mike has watched as his CEO counterparts have come in, implemented massive changes, and then leave a shattered mess of people and processes before moving on to their next career. Mike calls this the "blow in, blow up, and blow out" model of leadership. This is not how he wants to be remembered.

> What kind of LEGACY do you want to leave behind?

In other cases he has watched as charismatic leaders come in and build successful teams of people. These leaders say the right things and people begin to follow. As their influence grows, they successfully lead their companies with their charm and business savviness. He remembers one CEO who was headhunted from another organization and upon his departure left a gaping hole with no one to replace him. This charismatic leader was more concerned with building his portfolio than raising up others to fill his vacated position. Mike has always believed that using your charm to build yourself up while forgoing the investment in others along the way was not good leadership. This is not how he wants to be remembered. As he ponders these scenarios, Mike contemplates the legacy he is leaving behind. He envisions his future retirement party as he stands before his collogues and reminisces about the collective lessons learned from his time as CEO of Pure Energy. He scans the room and realizes that several people in the room began their careers with Pure Energy with entry-level positions and many are still with the company today.

He thinks about Diane who came in as an engineer fresh out of college and has worked hard ever since. She is always thinking outside the box which contributed to her developing two energy prototypes that changed the face of the company. When Mike invited her into the CORE leadership program, Diane had never thought much about succession planning or even her next steps. With the training she received from the CORE leadership program, Diane developed her personal portfolio and over time moved up within the company. Diane is now leading the entire engineering department and her readiness indicator shows that she could easily advance into the C-Suite at any moment.

He visualizes Jack who came into the company as a finance manager. Not long into his time at Pure Energy, Jack saw a need within the accounting department for a more secure and efficient system that would allow the company to save time and money. Eventually Jack led the entire accounting department through an overhaul that helped establish Pure Energy's accounting process as one of the best in the industry. While working on his CORE leadership profile, Jack realized his need for personal growth in the area of leadership. He connected with the local professional development program and received several personal and professional certifications. Three years ago when Rachel, the Chief Financial Officer, had to relocate to another state to take care of her ailing parents, Jack was promoted to CFO. Pure Energy did not skip a beat during this transition due to Jack's leadership qualifications.

Mike continues to look around the room in his mind and sees person after person who joined the Pure Energy team. Many have been promoted within the company due in large part to the CORE leadership program that benefited them both personally as well as professionally. The success of his employees stemmed from Mike's choice to think differently about how to build the kind of legacy that would outlast everyone.

Mike is startled from his daydream as his wife, Cheryl, comes into the den singing "Happy Birthday to You" and handing him a birthday card. Cheryl played a large role in Mike's decision to leave behind a legacy. She and Mike would have long talks about the future and how best to leave the company better than when they arrived. Early in his career, Mike had attempted to leave a legacy with limited success. Pure Energy was different.

Mike accepted the CEO position for Pure Energy fifteen years ago. He realized from the beginning that he would need to be fully intentional to become a true legacy maker. He started by thinking differently about everything within the business: leadership development, talent acquisition, a multi-generational workforce, and empowerment. Mike and his team realized that aside from the day-to-day operations they were also in the people-development business and would need to develop a leadership pipeline. They would need to enable the multi-generational workforce to feel empowered and to give them the tools necessary for success. Because he knew succession planning was actually about leadership development, several years ago Mike began looking for a system to help him raise up leaders within his company. What he found was a system that ultimately defined and generated the legacy he wanted to be remembered for long after his retirement party.

HOW WILL YOU BE REMEMBERED?

Everyone wants to be remembered for something. We all work hard in hopes of leaving a little piece of ourselves behind for others to emulate. No one wants to look back on their lives and realize that they left nothing behind of value. At the core of every single human being is the desire to know that what we do matters

> *"Carve your name on hearts, not tombstones. A legacy is etched into the minds of others and the stories they share about you."*
> —*Shannon L. Alder*

and how we live matters and what we accomplish matters. For business leaders, raising up others and helping them develop the skills to move forward and upward not only gives them the opportunity for growth but also gives them the chance to leave behind something that matters. Furthermore, the collective successes of those we foster is foundational to building our legacy. How to develop a leadership pipeline that will raise up new leaders and leave behind a viable legacy is a fundamental question that businesses both large and small need to ask. Will you be remembered as a legacy maker?

BECOMING A LEGACY MAKER

We can't answer the question of how to become a legacy maker until we first define what a legacy is. Having a legacy ensures that what you build, develop, train, and release will have meaning when you're gone. Legacy operates from a place of seeing the big picture and giving yourself the emotional energy to plan for the future while leveraging your current resources or assets. Companies spend little time thinking about legacy whether it be the legacy of the company or the leaders within the company itself. Building a legacy also requires the development of a multi-generational workplace which promotes generational synchronicity. Learning to see generations through the lens of stages of life instead of adhering to the generic generational stereotypes promotes a company's legacy.

Legacy makers realize that the time is now. Not only does a legacy maker understand the importance of developing a culture and ethos within an organization, they realize the added benefits of teaching their team about building a legacy. Walking your team through legacy leadership by getting to the CORE allows for a much clearer picture of the future in relation to your current talent pool and the current needs of your organization.

Leaving behind a legacy begins with you. It begins with the recognition that when you empower personal development, you begin to see empowered leadership. Understanding ourselves and our leadership capacity is the starting point for building an effective team. Once your team is flourishing, a legacy maker will begin to develop and promote leaders from within their organization which in turn will launch these new leaders to be part of building a legacy of their own. What are you currently doing within your organization to leave behind a legacy?

This book is written in two parts to help you think through the legacy you want to leave behind. Part one speaks to the different generations beginning with the Silent Generation through the up-and-coming Generation Z. These chapters will explore generational differences and how these differences show up within the workplace. It will guide you in creating a multi-generational, corporate environment that will help you successfully integrate these generations as you invest in their personal and professional development.

Part two describes the CORE Team Leadership Model I created through personal research that I used while working with several organizations to help them think through a leadership development pipeline by getting to the CORE of what's really important. Do you have what it takes to become a legacy maker?

PART 1
Exploring Generational Differences in the Workplace

1
LESSONS FROM THE TRADITIONALISTS
[BIRTH YEARS: 1929-1945]

"The greatest generation was formed first by the Great Depression.
They shared everything— meals, jobs, and clothing. It is, I believe,
the greatest generation any society have ever produced."
—Tom Brokaw

Traditionalists, also known as the Silent Generation, see the world differently. Growing up in the midst of the Great Depression and in the shadow of the WWII shaped the character of this generation. They learned growing up that children are to be seen and not heard. Traditionalists desire to be legacy makers because they have seen and experienced much in their lifetimes. This generation is retiring later and working longer for many reasons. The Silent Generation is the oldest generation in the workforce today and is still nearly 14 million strong. They are still shaking up the workplace with their fierce loyalty to their companies. They continue to challenge leadership with their industry knowledge and desire to see their organizations succeed.

This generation built a strong nation during some difficult times. They helped lay the foundation for future generations to experience everything from the American Dream to the freedoms we are so thankful for in our society today. This generation's influence in the workplace will likely remain long after they've retired.

HIERARCHICAL LEADERSHIP

Hierarchical leadership can best be explained as an organizational structure where power belongs to the position rather than an individual. This reduces the risk of an abuse of power by one person. This method of business leadership was inherited from this generation's military background. Many served in our nation's military where they learned quickly that those at the top were the brains and those at the bottom were the brawn. This type of leadership suited itself perfectly for the world of the traditionalist.

> HIERARCHICAL LEADERSHIP can best be explained as an organizational structure where power belongs to the position rather than an individual.

After the war, the two largest industries were manufacturing and farming. The traditionalists showed up for work, were shown what to do by the person in charge, and they would do the job. This led to a generation that is true to their word and one that follows through on their word. Trust and reliability are foundational for this generation. These traits helped define their career paths; you put in your time and work your way up the ladder. It has always been about loyalty and learning the systems to then be able to jump through the right hoops to be successful. The payoff in the minds of many traditionalists is when you finally arrive at the top of the ladder, then you are the one who gets to tell others what to do.

Hierarchical leadership has a place within our organizations still today though it will need to look different. Too often we simply throw out our differences rather than celebrating and recognizing the strengths each generation brings to the workplace. There is a leadership void within organizations today where vision casting needs to replace micro-management. Seeing the big picture that is marked with respect for rules, dedication, frugality, and loyalty will help our organizations continue to experience success and growth.

WORK ETHIC

Work ethic for the Silent Generation is of utmost importance. The traditionalists believe in hard work as their jobs are their livelihood. For the traditionalists, working at a job is not necessarily about doing something

> "The best way to learn is by doing. The only way to build a strong work ethic is getting your hands dirty."
> —Alex Spanos

that you are passionate about. It is more about survival. It is about feeding your family and making sure there is a roof over your heads. This intense work ethic has shaped their view of the workplace: you show up on time—if not early—work hard, and never miss a meeting. I recently talked with a traditionalist who told me that in his 34 years at his organization he only used two sick days. That fact clearly describes the work ethic of this generation.

At times this type of work ethic can draw out a negative response; however, if we put ourselves in the shoes of this generation and recognize how they view their jobs, we can see how the company has become so important to this generation. It is this understanding of the traditionalists that cultivates a respect for their experience and accomplishments. With their intense loyalty comes a sense of care and concern for the company and management. Traditionalists avoid participating in office drama and won't talk negatively about management personnel behind their backs. You can rest assured that if a traditionalist has a problem with their organization, they will respectfully voice their concerns to those in leadership above them.

FAMILY VALUES

This generation has deep family values. To a traditionalist, family equals happiness, hope, and a reason to get up and go to work even when the job is demanding, mundane, or unpleasant. Family values involve dinners

> "In modern life, we tend to forget family values because of the hectic schedule."
> —Mahesh Babu

around the table, a few inexpensive trips, and strolls through town or the neighborhood park. Though the faces of our families have changed tremendously, the desire to be connected to others still lives on. We can celebrate the diverseness of families and still look for ways to encourage healthy families within our communities.

Over the years I have learned some of my biggest life lessons from this generation. My desire to be a legacy maker is due in large part to two people: my father-in-law, Richard Linderer, and one of my dearest friends Sally Stancil. Both have passed on, yet the lessons I learned from each of them have shaped and inspired me to be a legacy maker.

RICHARD LINDERER

I was somewhat overwhelmed when I first met Richard Linderer. Richard was an intense man. When I was dating my wife, Stephanie, she gave me this warning before I met her father: "When you meet my dad, he is going to shake your hand. Just squeeze as hard as you can." When Stephanie's dad took my outstretched hand into his own, my hand literally disappeared. I squeezed as hard as I could as he looked me directly in the eye. He would become my father-in-law. I knew from that day on that this generation was about respect. Look them in the eye and squeeze their hand when you meet them. Respecting and treating people fairly is important and is something all generations should endeavor to live out in the workplace.

Richard was a retired police officer who worked part time as a federal marshal. The police department and the courthouse where he worked greatly esteemed him. He was a gunsmith and ran a successful gun-smithing business out of his shop behind his house. Many of the local police officers would bring their firearms to him to be repaired and cleaned. So many times we assume that the younger generations are more entrepreneurial; however, the work ethic of the traditionalists propels them to continue working long after retirement. This drive has led many traditionalists to become entrepreneurs.

Spending time with Richard, I saw a man who liked to work with his hands and could fix almost anything that he got his hands on. I remember times sitting in his shop and watching him take apart a broken electronic device. Although he would be talking with me about something, you could see he was really thinking about why this or that was not working. His mantra was "don't buy something new if you can fix what you have." This generation learned the importance of frugality because they lived through scarce times. The reality of the Great Depression tends to frame how this generation values money and resources. Traditionalists are extremely helpful within organizations when it comes to reusing and getting the most out of the resources available. They help us understand the value of things within the workplace. I encourage organizations to empower their traditionalists to help others understand these principles.

Richard eventually became not just my father-in-law but also my friend. He showed me how to change the oil in my car and how to sharpen a lawn mower blade. While he was teaching me how to fix small things around the house, he was also teaching me what responsibility looked like. Richard was a man who captured the essence of the Silent Generation through his respectful nature, his frugality, and his family values. He deeply loved his wife, Arlene, with the purest of love. He loved being around her, he loved helping her, and he always made time to be with her.

Richard also loved his grown children and would do just about anything for them. His face would light up whenever one of them would walk into the room. I remember days watching Richard sit around their swimming pool with the family. I remember enjoying family barbeques when, after we all filled up on hamburgers and potato salad, Richard would pull out his motorized ice cream maker that he engineered to crank the ice cream. I would admire him as he would sit by the ice cream maker with a look of pride all over his face. He was an example to me of the importance of family.

I will forever be different because of my time spent with Richard Eugene Linderer. I only wish that more people would have had the chance to know him. He was and will always be one of the most incredible men I have ever had the opportunity to know. Richard embodied many of the characteristic traits of the traditionalists: hard work, dedication, frugality, loyalty, and deep-rooted family values and respect for others. Our organizations have much to learn from this generation.

SALLY STANCIL

The funny thing about writing about my friend Sally is that she always teased me about how much I talked about her. I would call her on the phone and tell her I had spent the whole day teaching a class during which I had described her impact on my life. Her response was, "How do you talk about me all day?" Sally had a sense of humor and she would be laughing now if she knew I was writing about her in this book. Sally grew up in a wealthy doctor's home in Atlanta, Georgia. She had plenty of opportunity to allow her upbringing to cause her to think of herself more highly than others. Yet Sally embraced others and showed me the importance of thinking of others better than myself. When I first meet Sally, she was a 65 year-old widow who had one of the biggest hearts I have ever seen. She loved people well and she helped me see the value in all types of people. Every Wednesday for several years Sally and I would talk on the phone. She always asked how I was doing, how my family was doing, and then she would encourage me.

Sally enjoyed horse racing and supported all aspects of this equestrian performance sport, including the Race Track Chaplaincy of America. She not only supported this organization financially, but she would send them letters of encouragement and original poetry. Sally was an incredible poet. She captured the world as she saw it through her beautiful sonnets. There have been numerous times when I had been in a personal crisis or just down in the dumps when along came an email or letter with a poem inside from Sally. It was always exactly what I needed at that moment in my life. Few people in the world today understand encouragement like my friend Sally did.

Sally loved people well. She did not need to be the center of attention, but when she did speak most people listened. She operated from a place of depth and wisdom. I have personally benefited from sitting across the table from Sally, sharing a meal with her as she offered great wisdom to me. There are few people in the world with whom I feel completely safe; however, Sally was one person who I knew I could share anything with and she would continue to encourage me.

LEARNING THE LESSONS

The Silent Generation has much wisdom to offer within the workplace. We need to not lose sight of the way traditionalists embrace others and make others feel valued. They have given us a roadmap for how to see the world, and in many ways our organizations would not be where they are today were it not for their influence and leadership. Give them opportunities to share their unique perspective and capture their leadership lessons before it is too late. They challenge us to be the best we can be. Traditionalists like Richard and Sally are true legacy makers. They set the table beautifully for how to leave behind something that lasts.

2
THE BABY BOOMER MESSAGE
[BIRTH YEARS: 1946-1964]

"From now on we live in a world where man has walked on the moon.
It's not a miracle; we just decided to go."
—Tom Hanks

Roughly ten thousand people a day turned 65 years old in the United States in 2017. And not everyone who turns 65 is leaving a career and floating effortlessly away into retirement. This option, however, becomes much more appealing as baby boomers push on toward new upcoming adventures hovering over the horizon. Many boomers I talk to tell me they are just getting warmed up. They insist they are just coming into their own in the workplace. They are finding their leadership voice as they begin to look at how they can leave a legacy within their organizations.

According to a 2017 AARP article, entitled older workers remain on the job. Catherine Collinson, president of the Transamerica Center for Retirement Studies, says that many baby boomers are planning to work longer and retire at an older age partly for the income but also for enjoyment.

> Because the **BABY BOOMER GENERATION** is remaining longer in the workforce, finding ways to help them finish well is one of our most pressing situations today.

She adds that many people in this generation are still trying to make up for financial losses suffered in the 2008-09 recession.

"Many older workers are working because they have increasingly insecure sources of income, in the form of 401(k)s or IRAs or nothing at all besides Social Security," says Teresa Ghilarducci, a labor economist and director of the Schwartz Center for Economic Policy Analysis at the New School in New York.

According to Public Policy Institute, about 34.9 million people ages 55 and up were employed in February of 2017. Construction, private educational services, manufacturing, health care and mining all experienced job growth for workers of all ages. Because the Baby Boomer Generation is remaining longer in the workforce, finding ways to help them finish well is one of our most pressing situations today.

Boomers engage in the workforce with a mindset similar to the traditionalists. They see the big picture and desire to help add value of an organization. Many have worked their way into upper management or leadership within their companies. Because of being raised by traditionalists, the work ethic of baby boomers is characterized by loyalty and dedication to their jobs. They have a tendency to make long commitments to organizations and look toward retirement verses changing jobs or trying something new.

Through my time consulting and training others, I have had several opportunities to work alongside baby boomers. What always strikes me is the longevity that many from this generation have within their organizations. Because they are career focused, it's not uncommon for boomers to work for the same organization for 25, 30, even 40 plus years. Our organizations need to be gleaning and transferring the boomers' vast industry knowledge and their wide-ranged experiences in the pursuit of a multi-generational workplace.

As the baby boomers begin to think through the next five to fifteen years in the workplace, there are several questions to be answered in order for them to leave behind a legacy within their organizations.

HAVE YOU IDENTIFIED YOUR REPLACEMENT?

Every time I ask this question I am amazed at how many leaders have not thought this through whatsoever. There has been no thought given as to who is next to take their place. To give credit where credit is due, some organizations do a

> "We're here for a reason.
> I believe a bit of the reason is to
> throw little torches out to lead
> people through the dark."
> —Whoopi Goldberg

great job of succession planning and developing leaders along the way; however, the vast majority of leaders that I have encountered have not spent much time identifying their replacements. The reason for this is twofold: (1) a lack of job description and (2) a fear of losing their job to the person they are raising up to replace them.

Statistics show that people from almost every level within an organization don't really know what they were hired to do. Many organizations have done a poor job of helping employees understand and adhere to their job descriptions. How much of what you actually do is spelled out in your formal job description? How about the rest of your team? Do they know what is required of them? Many boomers never set up a succession plan because they have not slowed down enough to consider how to explain to someone within their organization what it is that they do.

Fear that the person raised up will do the job better is the second factor that can hinder the process of identifying a replacement. This fear of losing their job or wondering if the company will force them into early retirement is not something that only boomers face. All generations can struggle with the fear of raising up a leader who they perceive might outperform them which in turn can paralyze succession planning.

WILL THIS COMPANY OUTLAST YOU?

Many baby boomers who are in leadership within an organization struggle with the possibility that the company will not outlast them. They struggle with a lack of confidence that the company will be sustained when they are not making the day-to-day decisions. They pour their blood, sweat, and tears into their company and often worry about its future. This is the reason why sitting down and identifying who within your organization has what it takes to grow with your organization is so important.

If you want your company to outlast you, then it's up to you to find the right person to replace you. You have to be willing to take a chance on someone who might see things differently but who has the ability to take your organization and move it to the next level. Finding this person is not impossible; in fact, they might be closer than you think. Investing in and developing leaders within your organization can help ensure that your company outlasts you.

HOW ARE YOU PASSING ON YOUR INDUSTRY KNOWLEDGE?

One of the greatest tragedies in our organizations today is the amount of industry knowledge that walks out the door every time someone leaves a job either through retirement, a job transfer, or being let go. Organizations that recognize the importance of harnessing this knowledge from those nearing retirement age promote a solid cross-generational workplace. They foster a work environment where the older employees take time to transfer their knowledge and skills to those employees with less experience. Knowing what information to catalog can make passing the baton so much easier.

One organization I was consulting had several leadership team members who possessed between 30 and 40 years of industry knowledge. Much of their knowledge was simply in their heads and was not written down. As we started to explore the passing of the baton, we realized that much of this information was going to be lost in the transfer. We put a group together with the sole intent of capturing this industry knowledge using videos. The videos were then edited into 3-5 minute clips that where archived and made available on the company's internal web hosting. This became one of the leader's final projects and something that not only left a legacy but will continue to inspire generations to come. It will also enhance the organization's younger leaders as they learn to tell the story of their company's rich history.

WHAT CRITERIA DO YOU USE TO IDENTIFY LEADERS?

Many within the Baby Boomer Generation are now being tasked with identifying, empowering, promoting, and launching leaders within their organizations. The struggle most have with this task stems from an inconsistent radar for identifying and raising up those leaders. This lack of a clear process to identify new leaders causes many to just simply choose the person who has the most experience regardless of their leadership capability or skill set.

Think about your current leadership identification criteria within your organization. Once a leader is identified within your organization, how do you define what the next steps are for you and for the new leader? How do you communicate these next steps to all involved? Many leaders within organizations have never taken the time to have a conversation with an employee to let them know they have been identified as someone with potential for growth and a continued upward trajectory. Some organizations I have worked with have had seasoned leaders identify up-and-coming leaders but failed to let these individuals know. Having clear criteria for recognizing and developing leaders helps ensure you as a legacy maker when departing an organization.

Consider using a white board to mock up a strategy around how to identify leaders within your organization. What kinds of questions would you ask? How would you disseminate the information to all levels within the entire organization? How would you guarantee a buy-in from your entire team or organization?

WHAT IS YOUR EXIT STRATEGY?

It is important to notice that I ask this question using the word *strategy* rather than the word *plan* when talking about your exit. Exit plans are typically written in isolation or with a small select group of people. These exit plans are not necessarily shared with the entire organization. In contrast, an exit strategy is often written with more input from the organization and is frequently reviewed on an annual or semi-annual basis. This allows everyone to see that you have thought through what's best for the organization before leaving.

In preparing an exit strategy, outlining how your control will be released is one of the biggest questions to be answered. How will you empower people and not be the bottleneck in the process of your leaving? The ability to paint a picture around an exit strategy helps you to think through all the moving pieces and lets you know if any restructuring needs to occur. A solid exit strategy maintains continuity and stability within an organization.

A few years ago, I stepped away from an organization after being there less than a year. In the process of leaving, I created a 40-page exit strategy with the leadership team to ensure that the organization would continue to succeed. This exit strategy was employed throughout the organization and several amazing and needed transformations took place. I am convinced that a good exit strategy takes time and intentionality. A well-executed departure is an important part of the legacy you are leaving behind.

WHAT KIND OF MENTORING IS HAPPENING?

I am amazed by the number of people who know the value of mentoring and yet it's not happening. When many boomers in leadership hear the word *mentoring*, they think of hours and hours of conversations with a mentee who they hope will glean something of value and apply it to their work

> *"Colleagues are a wonderful thing —but mentors, that's where the real work gets done."*
> —Junot Diaz

life. Mentoring does take time; however, mentoring programs are incredibly important and there are several ways to implement them.

One-On-One Mentoring

For one-on-one mentoring to be fully effective, it must be a two-way mentoring process. The mentor is most usually the person with longevity or history in the organization. Although the mentor will be passing on industry knowledge, he or she seeks to understand how the mentee sees the organization. Being open to the perspective of the each generation, the mentor and mentee can learn ways in which both can work together better.

Speed Mentoring

This type of mentoring uses short, focused conversations about specific questions to transfer industry knowledge in a non-threatening way. Begin by compiling a list of questions to the mentees to get the conversations started. Each mentor will meet with a limited number of mentees. The advantage here is that each mentee will have the opportunity to meet multiple mentors in a short time. I have seen organizations do this over lunch once a month and the value of such a concentrated mentoring time can be seen throughout the organizations' productivity and retention; people stay where they feel they are growing and developing.

Group/Cohort Mentoring

This type of mentoring recognizes that people enjoy processing in a group setting with many heads and many voices. It allows you to interact with more employees in a shorter amount of time. The cohort mentoring model often has the mentee guiding the session and is based on a topic or a book. The mentor simply gets to participate as one who is senior in position but part of the mentoring cohort.

LISTEN TO THE MESSAGE

The baby boomer message is one of desiring to hand off what they know to the up-and-coming generations in the workplace. It's a message of living out what they learned growing up which was to share and to work together. This is a generation that grabbed hold of working hard because working hard shows that the job is important. They bring a spirit of optimism and teamwork. Although they grew up with an infrastructure that was not ready for a boom of babies, they labor in part to ensure that every person gets the opportunity to grow and develop. The boomer message is clear: people matter. Let's work together to find ways to convey this message in today's workplace.

3

GENERATION X: THE "WHO CARES" GENERATION
[BIRTH YEARS: 1965-1980]

"We've all been raised on television to believe that one day
we'd all be millionaires, and movie gods, and rock stars. But we won't.
And we're slowly learning that fact. And we're very, very pissed off."
—*Chuck Palahniuk*

Welcome to the generation that raised themselves. The generation that made the decision that they were going to look out for themselves and no one else. The generation that grabbed hold of cynicism which directly impacted their worldview. This generation has been described as the least parented and the least nurtured generation in our country's history. Now Generation X proudly wears their corporate distrust like a badge of honor as they shrug their shoulders with exasperation saying, "Who really cares anyway?" These four words sum up Generation X.

Generation X, also called the Squished Generation, is

> **A LATCHKEY KID** is defined as a child who is at home without adult supervision for some part of the day, especially after school until a parent returns home from work.

a unique cohort that has grown up with a complex and a chip on their shoulder from the beginning. Being part of a small generation squished between the boomers on one end and the millennials on the other would give most people a complex. Add a divorce rate that skyrocketed during the seventies and you begin to see why this generation grew up taking care of themselves with limited guidance from others. This generation realized early on that if they were going to be successful in the workplace then they would have to do whatever it would take to make that a reality.

With so many Gen Xers growing up in homes with absent parents due to divorce and the sharp rise of women entering the workforce, these children were sometimes referred to as the Latchkey Generation. A latchkey kid is defined as a child who is at home without adult supervision for some part of the day, especially after school until a parent returns home from work. Coming home to an empty house created a mindset that many from this generation still carry with them to this day. They ask, "If I don't care for myself, who is going to?" They grew up believing that their parents traded the role of parenting for their careers. Because the parents' jobs seemed more important, the latchkey kid became an adult who developed a suspect attitude toward the workplace and a need to know what's in it for them.

Although the tendency is to paint Generation X as having a silo mentality and as a generation that looks out only for themselves, one of the greatest attributes that arises from this generation is loyalty to friends. Because both parents worked during their formative years, Gen Xers' friends became their most prized possessions growing up. Family was busy with work; therefore, friends became their people of influence, help, and comfort. Caring for their friends so deeply growing up, Gen Xers have the ability to develop relationships within an organization and will often stay at a company to maintain their business relationships and friendships with co-workers. For many Gen Xers their relationships within an organization outweighs any other benefits they perceive the company offers them as employees.

THE GREAT GO-BETWEEN

One of the greatest gifts that Generation X brings to the workplace is the ability to understand the boomers and the millennials. This is a generation who has grown up with technology. Thus, the absence of fear of technology motivates them to learn how to use it to keep up with the changing times. This provides Gen Xers with a wide range of communication skills in the workplace today. This go-between generation has enough "tech speak" to engage with the Millennial Generation and to understand where these youngers are coming from, but also enough old school mentality to connect will with the boomers. This allows many from within Generation

X to be seen as trustworthy in both camps. I encourage organizations to use Gen Xers as the bridge builders when resolving misunderstandings among multiple generations in the workplace.

Because of their upbringing, many Gen Xers are willing to buck the system. It's not simply about asking questions of the organization due to mistrust; it runs far deeper with a desire to see change and a willingness to lead that change even if it's not popular. I often challenge the Gen X leader to use their angst for the good of the orga-

> *"My whole life has been about confronting cynicism."*
> —Cory Booker

nization and not against the organization. Some Gen Xers will strongly oppose the rules of an organization and focus on pushing hard on the company for change or to take down the company all together. This Gen X employee needs to be redirected and educated on the difference between a willingness to push back on the company or push back on the competition. This is one of the greatest leadership lessons this generation must tackle.

Many Gen Xers have the willingness and ability to be the first ones to think outside the box with a fresh look at how organizations can better themselves by putting people before the company instead of putting the company before the people. Since organizations exist because of people, Generation X is sensitive to keeping people at the forefront of the organization. They believe that the success of the organization is contingent on the success of its employees.

Now that Gen Xers have established a work history, they are thinking through several aspects of their careers based on the fact that many have between 15 and 25 years left until they reach retirement age. Gen Xers need to be ready to answer several questions as they make decisions regarding their future and their engagement within their organizations.

WHAT DO YOU BELIEVE ABOUT YOUR ORGANIZATION

A fundamental question for Gen Xers is to ask themselves what they believe about their organization. They need to ask themselves if they believe their organization cares more about people or more about itself and its existence. They need to evaluate their level of trust for their organization. Many times, the Gen Xer's distrust comes from seeing the company say one thing and then respond differently in their operating criteria. If the company says it embodies a culture of trust yet the executive team proves to be not trustworthy, a Gen Xer is likely to call out this hypocrisy within the leadership ranks.

A Gen Xer wants to know that the organization is not only trustworthy but solid when it comes to vision and values. I know of several Gen Xers who are constantly asking their companies to identify their vision and values not just in official verbiage but through actions and behaviors. They don't want you to *tell* them how to live as an employee of the organization but to *show* them how to live an as employee. They are more willing to fully engage in a company that not only talks about having a culture of trust but one that backs it up with actions. This generation can get bogged down by their skepticism but are savvy nonetheless.

WHAT ARE YOU DOING TO HELP DRIVE THE ORGANIZATION FORWARD?

Gen Xers can get caught up in playing devil's advocate and forget about finding ways to propel the company forward. Helping Gen Xers identify their primary buy-in and concern for the organization is important and can help to settle their restless spirit. What contributions are they making to the betterment of the company?

I worked with one Gen Xer who realized that she was living with a critical spirit toward her organization. Whenever she was asked about her company she found she was always telling people about the negative things. There were several instances when people would respond by saying, "Wow! It sounds like you don't appreciate your job much." She finally realized that her attitude toward her job was one of cynicism and criticalness toward her organization. She decided she needed to start asking what she was doing to help drive her organization forward with her position. Her first reality check came as she began to see how her critical attitude was hurting her ability to make a difference at her job. She took a gratitude challenge and every day for 30 days she shared with others how her company was having a positive impact on her life and career.

To do this she had to find ways in which she was either helping the company with her job by pushing the company forward or contributing to its ongoing success, not tearing it down. She started by being more of a team player. She more fully engaged in the weekly staff meetings and came prepared to participate. She also shared with others how she was looking for ways to purposefully be more collaborative and less siloed in her approach to teams. This took being intentional but over time she realized that she was actually helping grow the organization. Her ultimate recognition was how her critical attitude had been contributing to the sickness of her organization instead of to its health. She also was able to see how her poor attitude would eventually tear down her company to the point that even her position would no longer exist.

HOW DO YOU HELP YOURSELF STANDOUT FROM OTHERS?

Many within the Generation X cohort have spent plenty of time separating themselves from the pack. How do the Gen Xers help themselves to be noticed or to be a standout? This has less to do with the hard skills and more to do with the soft skills necessary to interact in a healthy way with others in the workplace. Just as with the boomers, a strong work ethic and the ability to see the world for what it is instead of going around with a chip on their shoulder are two of the most valuable traits that can help set Gen Xers apart in the workplace.

> "Saying no can be the ultimate self-care."
> —Claudia Black

Many within Generation X struggle with a frequent inability to say no because they so badly want to be appreciated and to stand out from the crowd. When you grow up with both parents working or grow up in a broken home, you find that you simply want someone to notice you. When you find that someone who does notice you, you tend to work really hard for them. But just working hard for attention can turn into an unhealthy approach to your career as saying no becomes more and more difficult. Although finding ways to separate yourself is a key to continued growth and development, if pursued by rarely saying no, it can lead to burnout. When you learn the power of the word "no," a whole new world emerges.

I am from the Generation X cohort and this was one of my biggest struggles in the workplace. At the core of who I was, I had an inability to say no. I felt like I was letting people down or that people would think less of me if I said no. This led to a work life that was severely one-sided to the point that I was working eighty to ninety hours a week and neglecting my family in the process. This inability to say no was causing fractured relationships both within my home and my workplace.

As parts of my life started to unravel, I began to explore my inability to say no. What was it rooted in? For me it came from the place of wanting my parents' affection but they were always too busy. Looking back I can see that I basically raised myself. I got my first job when I was fourteen years old. My boss pulled me aside one day and said, "You are a really hard worker." In that moment, I felt like someone noticed me for the first time. It felt like I had just come out of the darkness into the light; therefore, I worked really hard for this boss in hopes he would keep noticing me.

I carried this deep need to be noticed with me to every job. This fed an inability to say no which grew over time. I found myself saying yes to someone even when I meant no. Living this way ultimately sent me to a counseling center where I began to work through why I couldn't or didn't say no. I now call myself a recovering "yes-man." I still have a tendency to say yes too often even when it would serve me best to say no. But I am choosing to live in the reality that freely saying no leads to freely saying yes; I have the freedom to say no when appropriate which in turns frees me up to say yes to those things I really want or need to do. Many Gen Xers resonate with this desire to be seen and for many it's born out of good intentions; however, not kept in check it can lead to placing your identity in what you do instead of who you are.

If you are a leader of a Gen Xer, it might be helpful to have the conversation with them about what they are saying yes and no to. It wasn't until someone shined a light on this subject for me that I was aware of what was happening behind the scenes of my life. It was only then that I was able to see that my strong desire to be seen stemmed from my childhood. Understanding the baggage we carry forward from our childhood can lead to a new-found freedom as we learn how not to let these wounds own or define us.

HOW WILL YOU MOVE INTO THE C-SUITE?

For many within the ranks of Generation X, the time for stepping into a senior leadership role within their organization is rapidly approaching. They have finished the hard work of postgraduate degrees coupled with the necessary experience to prepare themselves for the moment when a door opens to a C-Suite position. Outside of postgraduate studies, what are you currently doing to prepare yourself for the C-suite? What other books are you reading? How are you networking? How are using your skills within the organization to prepare for what's next?

Find a mentor

At this point in your career, I strongly recommend finding a mentor within your industry who can help you develop the leadership skills needed to move up within your organization. (See "The Boomer Message" for more on mentoring and its benefits.)

Find a coach

Another great way to prepare for movement into the C-Suite is through executive coaching. Coaching gives you access to a personalized growth plan and the opportunity to develop skills that you don't use in your current job but may be necessary for your next role. There are several great resources on the topic of executive coaching and personal growth plans. One that I highly recommend is The Complete Leader, a 14-month EMBA-style leadership development program. This leadership program includes monthly coaching sessions and gives the participants some of the best hands-on learning and coaching available today. (For more information go to www.thecompleteleader.org.)

WHAT DO YOU WANT TO BE KNOWN FOR?

How Gen Xers answer this question helps set the stage for the direction of their personal development, leadership development, and trajectory for how they will get there. As Generation X enters into the prime of their work lives, they will need to ask themselves if they want to be legacy makers. In many ways, how this generation answers this question of becoming a legacy maker or not helps solidify the path they will take for growth.

According to Gary Keller in his book *The ONE Thing*, nothing just happens. You have to spend time focusing on it and being intentional about what you want to be known for. If you want to be known as an innovative leader, what are you doing now to foster innovation? If you want to be known as a transparent leader, what are you doing now to foster transparency? If you want to be known as collaborative player, what are you doing now to foster collaboration? Whatever you want to be known for, you have to begin to move in that direction. It won't happen overnight but if you work at it and stay focused you will be amazed at the results. Eventually what you want to be known for will be what people will attach to your name.

Deciding what kind of legacy you want to leave behind is essential to propelling yourself forward into what's next of your career. Take time to fill in the blanks:

I want to be known for _____.

To make it happen, I am willing to do_____.

This is the first step on your way to becoming the leader you want to become.

Despite their skepticism, Generation X with their savviness and loyalty will lead the way in people development. They shoot for the stars in making things happen and will be the first through the wall when things don't go the way we thought. They are in an intense growth phase, and if we help them discover their potential, our organizations will flourish because of what they bring to the table.

4
THE MILLENNIAL "GENERATION ME" MYTH
[BIRTH YEARS: 1981-2000]

"Millennials don't want to be managed, they like to be led,
coached and mentored. This generation is on fire and ready to go.
Are you ready to change the world?"
—Farshad Asl

Isn't it easy to blame the millennials for killing everything? Aren't those entitled millennials the ones causing all the problems within our economy and wrecking our companies? If the millennials would just be a little less entitled and little more grateful and take a learning posture within their jobs, our organizations would be much more successful. I hear this sentiment or something like it many times when I am talking with leaders about the Millennial Generation within the workforce. Many organizations today have a tendency to blame the Millennial Generation for their "me-centric" attitude. But is this generation really to blame?

What if it's less about entitlement and more about a generation that has been constantly challenged to go for it and a mindset that believes the sky is the limit? Keep in mind that many millennials are the children of baby boomer parents. Boomers grew up in a world where the infrastructure was not ready for the boom of babies. Boomers were expected to be mature and hard working with minimal interaction with their parents. In essence, boomers had to figure it out along the way, enduring countless struggles and disappointment. This caused many boomer parents to consistently rescue their millennial children from life's hardships and to continually set them up for success. This rescue-style method of child rearing has led to many people believing that millennials are entitled.

> Keep in mind that many millennials are the CHILDREN OF BABY BOOMER parents.

FROM ENTITLEMENT TO ENGAGEMENT

Looking at the Millennial Generation with fresh eyes will allow one to recognize that this generation is not asking for a handout just like they were not asking for first-place trophies fifteen years ago. What they are looking for is engagement. They want the opportunity to get involved with something that they care about and that will actually make a difference in the world. The Millennial Generation watched their parents work for organizations and give their souls to corporate America only to lose their identities in their work and then wonder what is most important to them. Watching your parents go through a corporate identity crisis can lead to a generation that views organizations from a perspective of wanting to assure that they don't come to the end of their lives and wonder the same thing. They want to know that their current contribution matters and promotes a difference in the workplace both locally and at a global level.

Millennials are a team-oriented generation who find working collaboratively leads to better engagement versus division and competition. Many millennials also believe that you can find your own voice in the midst of collaboration which they say helps them be more effective in their jobs. This teamwork mindset is not just for the workplace as millennials enjoy devoting many aspects of their lives to giving away what they have learned to others.

Millennials want to make their time count. Their engagement is not necessarily a 9-to-5 business. It's a 24/7 operation without being limited to the standard workday perimeters. Some of the leaders in organizations I have worked with tell me that they don't feel their millennial employees have the same buy-in as other employees. It is usually less about the millennial's buy-in and more about work-life balance. Millennials strive for the type of work-life balance that gives them flexibility in where, when, and how they work. They will choose to work on a project at 2 AM because they want to try out a new idea. Many millennials during school found their prime working time and would work their class schedules around this time frame. They have figured out how to make the most of their time each day and desire to engage in their jobs when their minds are truly alive whether at 2 AM or 2 PM. They will give far more than 40 hours a week to their jobs but if forced too tightly into a routine they will rebel and push back. Because the Millennial Generation realizes that everything could be gone tomorrow, it is vitally important to them to fully engage in the world today.

THE TRAGEDY OF 9/11

Although we all were affected by the tragic events of September 11, 2001, no generation has seen the repercussions played out as much as the Millennial Generation. The older millennials were in their formative years at that moment in history and had to make sense of terrorism at home. This was a generation that for the first time realized that maybe they were not as safe as they thought they were.

On the heels of 9/11 many older millennials went straight to their local military offices and signed up to serve our country. This influx of millennials into the military has also played a role in the shaping of this generation. It demonstrated a new wave of patriotism. It catapulted this generation to become more globally mindful. As a result, I have encountered several millennials who make the most of the opportunities in front of them here at home and abroad for they realize that tomorrow is not a guarantee.

The fear that encapsulated this generation still has an impact on the workplace today. Many millennials have made decisions to move to smaller communities they deem as safer for their families. One millennial I talked with recently told me that even though he was a senior in high school at the time of the 9/11 attacks, he still makes life decisions based on that event. He has taken jobs and turned down jobs based on how high or low the company's profile is regarded and on how safe he perceives the community to be.

TECHNOLOGY EVERYWHERE

The Millennial Generation has grown up with technology. This is a generation who has a hard time remembering life without cell phones, iPads, and laptop computers. The Millennial Generation has embraced technology and believes that technology can ultimately lead to making our lives easier and help us in the work arena as well.

It's been said that most millennials don't read the instructions when the get a new piece of technology. Instead they will just begin to play around with it until they figure it out, resulting in discovering ways to better use the technology. Many millennials have been responsible for new innovations and applications simply from spending time using the technology and mastering it without the instructions.

> "We have become so preoccupied in clicking, capturing and caging memories that we have forgotten to live them first."
> —Mitali Meelan,
> Coffee and Ordinary Life

Just google it! I can't tell you how many times I have heard this phrase from a millennial. I will ask a question on how to do something and they will reply, "I don't know. Just google it!" This reliance on the Internet has allowed millennials to harness the power of knowledge at their fingertips and use it to their advantage. If something is not working, a millennial knows that someone somewhere has created a video or a hack on how to fix the problem; they just have surf the web and find it. This readily available information is great when you need a YouTube video to fix your iPad or iPhone. Overusing technology, however, can contribute to a decline in critical-thinking skills, making troubleshooting without Google more difficult for some millennials. I have worked with several companies to help them write policies that define the appropriate usage of technology in the workplace to promote skills in problem-solving and analysis.

Many millennials often find ways to harness technology to become better at their jobs which can save their companies time and resources, ultimately saving their organizations money. When asked for ideas and suggestions on how to use technology to harness a company's resources, many millennials are more than happy to share their job hacks and technology boosters with their leaders.

EMERGING ADULTHOOD

Adulthood has been defined by these five benchmarks: (1) completing school, (2) leaving home, (3) becoming financially independent, (4) marrying, and (5) starting a family. A person was considered to be an adult once he or she reached four or five of these benchmarks. In 1960 77% of all women and 65% of all men had reached four out of five by the age of 30. In 2010 only 13% of all women and only 10% of all men had reached four out of five by the age of 30. Why this sharp decline? According to Jeffery Arnett, a psychology professor at Clark University in Massachusetts, our country is experiencing a new phase of life between adolescence and full adulthood lasting roughly from ages 18-25 that he termed "emerging adulthood." Arnett coined the term to describe the radical delay of full adulthood taking place within this Millennial Generation and describes the prolonged period of exploration during a person's late teens to their mid-twenties.

Arnett believes that because many millennials have such a great relationship with their parents, they are making decisions to live at home longer and do things like pay off college debt or save for a larger down payment on a first home. Some millennials just desire to travel and see the world before putting down roots.

Emerging adulthood has implications in the workplace as many millennials are looking for an opportunity to do something that has meaning rather than simply accepting a job for a paycheck. By living at home, these millennials can afford to make less income without a rent payment hanging over their head each month. This allows them to be more particular when choosing an organization to work for. When I am consulting businesses on their millennial retention rate, I ask them what makes their organization stand out from the rest. I encourage these companies to seriously ask themselves what onboarding techniques they have in place to attract and retain millennials. The following questions are on the hearts and minds of many millennials and how they answer these questions can give business leaders ways to engage with current and future millennial employees.

WHAT ARE YOU PASSIONATE ABOUT?

"Passion" can sometimes be a buzzword, but it is something that every generation must find. In his book *The ONE Thing*, Gary Keller guides you through discovering what you are truly passionate about. Give this book a read if you are struggling with identifying your personal passion. The Millennial Generation uses their passion as a guiding principle or North Star for their lives. They are constantly asking themselves if what they're

> If a millennial FINDS THEIR PASSION within your organization, you will have a committed employee in your workforce.

currently doing is something they truly want to be doing. If it's not, they will begin to look for another job. Millennials see their job and passion through the same lens; they are not about to doing something for a third of their lives that they are not passionate about. Millennials are serious about the passion question and are constantly looking for ways to answer it.

If a millennial finds their passion within your organization, you will have a committed employee in your workforce. They will be excited to go to work and will engage in the workplace with zeal. Exploring passion with your millennial employees is one of the ways in which you can make sure you have the right players on your team. Remember this generation engages differently with the world around them; it's less about a paycheck and more about purpose.

WHAT DO YOU WANT TO BE KNOWN FOR?

It's amazing how many people don't actually know what they want to be known for. They haven't stopped long enough to think about what type of legacy they are leaving behind.

As a professor at one of the local universities, I am constantly challenging students to think through this question. I have them do an activity designed to get them to think about their life goals and the values that actually embody those life goals. I give students a deck of cards that have different values printed on them, such as authenticity or balance. The value cards are laid down face up with the values showing. I instruct them to turn over all value cards except for the top ten values that they see in their lives on a daily or weekly basis. Next, they turn over five more cards so that their top five values are left. We then talk about how these five values begin to shape what they want to be known for. Then they turn over two more cards, leaving just the three most important values showing. We discuss how these are the guiding principles that govern how they see the world. Finally, I have them choose the single most important value that they defend to the rest of the class. I then ask each student, "If you were to live by this one value for the next thirty days, would people say that this value defines who you are already or would they say you're acting differently and why?

What do you want to be known for? Answering this question is foundational for the Millennial Generation. This will become a building block for them as they move forward into their careers. Helping them work through what they want to be known for can also help them understand their passions which ultimately leads to attracting and retaining passionate, purpose-filled millennials.

WHERE DO YOU SEE YOURSELF IN FIVE YEARS?

This is a must-have conversation with your millennial employees after they have had the opportunity to experience your culture. Upwards of 65% of millennials are currently looking for another job. Millennials jump from job to job for a variety of reasons such as a strained relationship with their boss or feeling like

> *"Follow your dreams and use your natural-born talents and skills to make this a better world for tomorrow."*
> —Paul Watson

they don't advance their company's mission. The number one reason a millennial leaves a job, however, is when they perceive their job is lacking a challenge to align with their passion.

Millennials thrive on a challenge as they have grown up in environments where finding answers to their questions or learning something new was part of the norm. They enter the workplace with an expectation that they will be challenged in new ways and struggle when their jobs don't continually provide it. One millennial I worked with told me about a new job in which it took her the full eight hours to complete her tasks. Five months into the job she could get everything done in less than two hours. She had automated and used technology to her advantage. After explaining to her boss that she was bored and that her skills and talent were no longer being used, her boss gave her meaningless busy work instead of pivoting her into a new role. She left this organization after only seven months, finding a job in another industry. It is vitally important to give millennials the opportunities to be challenged in the workplace. It was a great loss to the organization because she is a high-performing millennial.

When you discover where your millennial employees see themselves in five years, you will be able to better gauge their buy-in with your company. It will provide insight into the level of challenge these employees perceive in their current roles. Are they comfortable telling you what is and isn't working for them? Do they need to explore a new role? Helping them find their sweet spot that is both challenging and rewarding will boost your company's retention of its millennial employees.

WHAT SKILLS SHOULD YOU BE FOCUSING ON TO DEVELOP?

Facilitating the millennial employee to think through their skill set and how to continue to develop themselves is another way of retaining top millennial talent. When companies invest in the development of its millennials, they set them up for continued success. For a millennial, a clear path for growth and development needs to make them feel empowered not only by expanding their knowledge base but also by helping them see how they can make a difference with their newly acquired skills. They want to know that their work and their company has meaning beyond their paycheck. Coaching a millennial needs to encompass both their job as well as their life outside of the workplace.

When a company seeks to develop the entire employee, retention rates go up. Invite your millennials into the conversation on how to develop and achieve their goals. There are many different assessments both online and in-class training programs that identify exactly what type of skills are needed as well as how to develop those skills.

HOW CAN YOU INCREASE YOUR SELF-AWARENESS?

It's been said that one of the most promotable skills in the workplace is self-awareness. Self-awareness is the ability to understand your inner feelings, desires, and motives and how you come across to others. A lack of self-awareness rather than feeling entitled is one of the main reasons the Millennial Generation is often labeled as "Generation Me."

Being self-aware at work is executing on your responsibilities in a timely manner. You ask thoughtful questions to ensure clarity of your tasks. When you make a mistake in the process, take a step back, readily own your mistake, and keep moving forward. When the process is finished, you move onto the next thing. Being aware of how you come across to others can help you identify the weaknesses in your character that you need to work on.

Many younger employees as well as people at all levels within the organization are still learning this concept. There are numerous ways to increase your self-awareness. Make a commitment to learning more about yourself by taking a personality test. The TRACOM Group Social Styles Model is a good starting place. Ask for informal feedback while discussing professional development with your boss or other member of your team. Introspection and seeking out recreation can help you be more in tune with yourself when you resume your job duties. Learning self-awareness can go a long way to see real lasting change in our workplaces today.

STOP BELIEVING THE MYTH

I have had the opportunity to work with millennials for many years, and I consider the "Generation Me" label to be a myth that we all must stop believing. Leaders, as you seek to not only learn from your millennial employees but empower them to believe in themselves, you will attract and retain these talented young people who are walking in and out of your organizations every day. Millennials, as you seek to take a learning posture and to develop new skills, you will successfully navigate your career and continue to crush the "Generation Me" myth.

5
READY OR NOT, HERE COMES GENERATION Z
[BIRTH YEARS: 2001-present]

*"The big difference between this generation and others
is the fact that kids today carry personalized computers around with them
in their pockets all the time."*
—David Bell

Meet the newest generation. They are coming in full force whether we like it or not. Statistics pertaining to the size of Generation Z vary due to different beginning and ending dates for each generation; however, it is estimated at 69 million members. This upcoming generation is changing how we do things on almost every front. There is not much information about this young generation online so much of my research is home based. I have two Gen Z sons living in my home, and I interact with them and their friends on a consistent basis. Most of the information I am presenting in this chapter is based on my hypothesis from the research that I have done both personally and with other colleagues; it is truly in its infancy stage. Although the conversation about Gen Z is evolving, my background in generational trends may yield a higher degree of accuracy in the following predictions and descriptions of this new generation.

WHAT'S IN A NAME?

Generation Z has not settled on a name. According to sociologists, a generation name takes root when a generation begins to refer to themselves as being from a particular generation. Generation Z is not convinced of their name at the present time. Several names have been used to describe

> This group will be AMERICA'S LAST to see a Caucasian majority and, probably for this reason, be highly open to diversity.

this generation, such as Post-Millennials and iGeneration (a referral to the generation growing up with a smartphone in hand).

Another name that is gaining traction is Pluralist Generation or plurals. Matthew DeBord wrote an article about this generation and said, "This group will be America's last to see a 'Caucasian majority' and, probably for this reason, be highly open to diversity. Sounds good, but they'll also be 'the least likely to believe in the American Dream.'" This name believe it or not is gaining popularity among this generation as they see themselves as racially, ethnically, and religiously diverse.

My favorite name comes from a survey from MTV that asked a thousand 13- and 14-year-olds what they wanted their generation to be called. The winning name? The Founder Generation. This new generation is looking to find themselves separate from the millennials. They are about rebuilding a new society with new rules. Whatever name they choose to call themselves, how we react and relate to them is going to be important for the success of our organizations.

A TRUE MELTING POT

Given the changing face of our communities, we know that this generation is growing up in one of the most diverse environments our country has ever seen. Statics show that by 2020 there will not be a dominant culture in the United States; we will truly be a melting pot. Growing up in a melting pot of diversity has catapulted Generation Z to becoming the most diverse and inclusive generation yet. This generation may just lead the way in helping organizations embrace and manage the ever-increasing diversity within the workforce.

IT'S A SMALL WORLD AFTER ALL

Generation Z is the first generation to be digital natives. They can't remember a time without the Internet, smartphones, and social media. This exposes them to many different cultures

"Generation Z are like millennials on steroids."
—Dan Schawbel

worldwide with instant access to what's going on in the world as far outside of their immediate families and friends as they want to go. Gen Zers will be the generation that leads our organizations toward a brighter future because of their inclusive mindset. They are open to seeing the world from another perspective and are accustomed to looking for a third option. Generation Z will help us think through a third option when it comes to problem-solving due to their international interactions via the World Wide Web. They can more readily see a colorful world of possibilities versus simply one way.

FROM PEN PALS TO LIVE STREAMING

When I was in elementary school and even into middle school, my classmates and I had pen pals. We would actually use pencil and paper to write letters to our pen pals. In elementary school, we wrote letters to students from somewhere else in the United States. In middle school our pen pals were from another country. The best Friday afternoons were the ones when our teacher would say to the class that our letters had arrived. We would learn about how young people our same age from other cultures lived.

Today this generation is literally streaming live. There are virtual learning classrooms that connect students via technology to other classrooms of students from around the country and even from around the world. And live streaming doesn't stop at education. Many Gen Zers are playing games and having conversations in real time with other young people their own age from other countries. Xbox and PlayStation provide a platform for young people to converse with the person they are playing a game with in real time. This technology gives Gen Zers the ability to connect with people around the world and has fostered all sorts of learning opportunities. It has also exposed them to online predators and has given them a false sense of security.

WELCOME SCREENAGERS

Generation Z has spent more time in front of smartphone screens, computer screens, and television screens which has been blamed for a decrease in empathic conversational skills. Social scientists have just begun to study the effects of screen time on the social interactions of today's young people. They have determined that the more hours

"Whenever I'm bored, I can always find something to do on my phone."
—Male, 17

"I only watch Netflix."
—Female, 16

a young person spends looking at a screen, the more difficult it becomes for them to engage with others away from their screen in a meaningful and healthy way. It's not surprising then that Gen Zers would prefer having a digital conversation rather than face-to-face dialogue. This has raised concerns for this generation's mental health as overuse of smartphones, social media, and gaming may lead Gen Zers to feel isolated.

Entertainment for this generation can easily be a solo activity. Many Gen

Zers do not watch standard cable television. They prefer to binge-watch television shows that they stream on their individual smartphones or laptop computers. There was a time when families sat down and watched television or movies together. That reality is now waning as family time is beginning to be defined by each person viewing their own electronic device while being "together" in the same house at the same time.

Due to this generation's aptitude for computer touchscreens, many retailers have automated their point-of-sale machines with touchscreens as seen with self-checkout lines. Other examples include airport self-service kiosks and even select restaurant menu boards. All to say that this generation's information is literally at their fingertips.

As video gaming has gained in popularity, many of this industry's innovations have made their way into other areas in our society. Several branches of the armed forces are now piloting unmanned aerial vehicles, guiding bomb defusal robots, and directing other battlefield equipment using Xbox-type controllers. While this harnesses a generation's aptitude for gaming, there is a concern that young military personnel may more easily disconnect themselves from the real lives that are being taken while using gaming controls to fly drone into a battlefield. This is something the military is aware of, and they are working hard to help Generation Z understand that it's not just a game.

KNOCKING AT THE WORKFORCE DOOR

While millennials are about striving for passion, meaning, and balance in their jobs, Gen Zers are about putting money and job security at the top of their job lists. Why is this? Ever wonder how the Great Recession (officially lasting from December 2007 until June 2009) impacted and shaped this generation? It was during this recession that this generation experienced mom and dad losing jobs, their homes being foreclosed on, and being uprooted for a parent's new job or having to move in with grandparents. We often forget about the children in the midst of this time, but many had to leave schools and friends as well as endure the hardships associated with loss of income and housing instability. There are still families who have not fully recovered from the effects of the Great Recession. Some people are still underemployed or are house poor with little disposable income to live on.

It is understandable that Gen Zers will be far more interested in the longevity and stability of a company. They will be asking hard questions of organizations even for entry-level positions in order to gain confidence in a company's future presence. They will

> GAMIFICATION is another tool employers are using now to connect with Generation Z.

be about thriving and surviving in the workplace. Most likely they will be long-term employees if the company is fair, honest, and equitable. Trust in the viability of an organization's product or mission will be key for a Gen Zer to get onboard. Developing high school internships is one good way for organizations to connect with the Gen Zers who are knocking at the door of the workforce. Because this tech savvy generation is starting to build their careers in high school, those companies that offer internships help solidify their brand as well as stay competitive in today's marketplace.

Gamification is another tool employers are using now to connect with Generation Z. Gamification is the application of common game-playing elements to other areas of learning, education, job hiring, or on-the-job training. It is now being used as an online marketing technique to boost a person's engagement with a company's product or service. Because this generation is so focused on playing with their smartphones and game consoles, it is advantageous for organizations today to begin using gamification when designing their application and hiring process. This strategy taps into the Gen Zer's ability and enjoyment to engage with an online presence.

MAKE READY FOR GEN Z

The conversation about Generation Z is happening now; however, there is much more that can and will be written about this generation. As the next several years unfold, we will glean insight and understanding into how Gen Zers see the world and engage with the workplace. Ready or not, here they come.

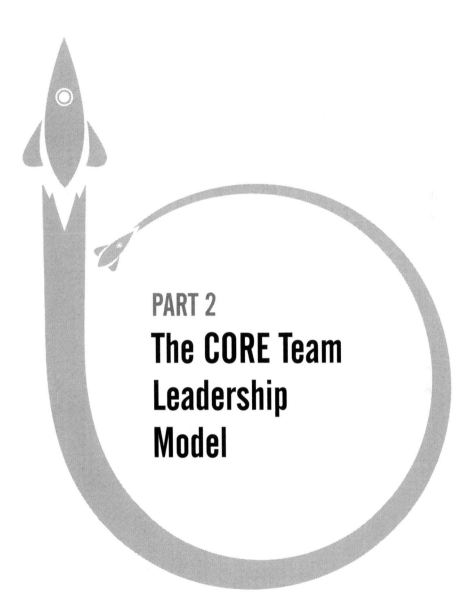

PART 2

The CORE Team Leadership Model

6
GETTING TO THE CORE

"Winning companies win because they have good leaders who nurture
the development of other leaders at all levels of the organization."
—*Noel Tichy*

t was statistician George Box who famously said, "All models are wrong, but some are useful." I agree with Mr. Box's statement and will lay out a model in this chapter that is useful for the advance of a leadership culture within organizations. The following pages contain research from my dissertation on developing a leadership model that has longevity where a leader can leave behind a legacy instead of a gaping hole.

My research was completed over a nearly two-year span through the lens of organizational development. I employed a qualitative research method as I went about my study. Qualitative research is primarily a method of inquiry. It is used to gain an understanding of underlying reasons, opinions, and motivations. It provides insights into the problem or helps to develop ideas or hypotheses for potential quantitative research. Qualitative research is also used to uncover trends in thoughts and opinions and to dive deeper into the problem. Qualitative data collection techniques can be unstructured or semi-structured. Common methods include focus groups (group discussions), individual interviews, and participation/observation.

Once I completed my research, I knew that the model needed to be implemented and thoroughly studied in real-world settings. I have spent the last six years working with for-profit and nonprofit organizations, helping them implement this leadership model. This model has evolved greatly from my initial research; therefore, my hope is that this book will further that research while assisting other organizations as they think through a culture of leadership development.

INTRODUCING THE CORE TEAM LEADERSHIP MODEL

The purpose of my dissertation was to show how a group of individuals, the CORE team, working together can bring about a holistic change to the face of an organization and become legacy makers. I use the acronym CORE throughout the book to refer to a proposed model of empowering and inspiring leadership: Collaborative Objective to Raise up

CORE:
C: Collaborative
O: Objective to
R: Raise up and
E: Empower

and Empower.

In each of the subsequent chapters, we will take a closer look at each one of the elements of the CORE Team Leadership Model. How do we work *collaboratively* among the generations? How do we clearly define an *objective* so we know where we are going and how we will get there? What does it mean to *raise up* leaders within our organizations? And once we have raised them up, how do we *empower* them in ways that will prepare them for what is next in their personal and professional development?

The CORE team's main objective is to cultivate a continual influx of fresh leadership by understanding and seizing the opportunity of multi-generational teams within the workplace. The CORE Team Leadership Model emphasizes the development of leaders within an organization and encourages emerging leaders to step into leadership roles. A CORE team that is multi-generational and vision-centric can operate effectively within the realm of leadership development and bring longevity to the entire organization.

The ultimate goal of the CORE Team Leadership Model is to see organizational vision sustained while releasing new leaders who have the ability to lead within their individual areas of giftedness or expertise. It is paramount to find ways to move away from person-centered leadership into a team-based approach centered on a set vision where each team member operates from his or her strengths. This vision-centric model promotes sustainability in the long term and allows for leaders to flourish as well as avoid burnout. The CORE Team Leadership Model allows for the eventual smooth transition of leadership to the next generation and envisions a truly multi-generational workplace.

IT STARTED WITH SCIENCE

This journey began while I was looking at my son's science homework. I noticed a picture of an atom (see Figure 1.1) on one of his homework pages. In that moment, I began to see how leadership teams could actually be mapped out in a similar way. As I stared at the atom's nucleus, I could see an organization developing leaders from within instead of the standard approach of looking for the next great hire from the outside. Many organizations have hired an outside individual at the top of their field only to find that he or she destroys their current team dynamics. Being a legacy

Fig. 1.1

maker is about developing your team now to launch new leaders from *within* your organization. If you are developing your team now, you are watering the seeds of success for what they need to mature into those future leaders.

In an atom, the function of the nucleus is two-fold: controlling what happens within a given atom and containing the DNA or blueprint of the purpose of a particular atom. The nucleus is the membrane-enclosed organelle found within the core of a cell. This nucleus or core section of the atom contains a cell's genetic material. It contains everything that organism needs to survive. Similarly, if you develop your employees, they will also have everything they need to survive; if done correctly, not just survive but thrive in your organization.

> "You gain strength, courage and confidence by every experience in which you really stop to look fear in the face. You must do the thing you think you cannot do."
> —Eleanor Roosevelt

The nucleus of the atom also houses both protons and neutrons with the electrons, the negatively charged subatomic particles, orbiting around the nucleus. All of these are working together to create the ideal environment for the atom to survive. This is an elementary look at an atom; however, in that moment I began to see how teams could be developed from within an organization. To mimic the atom and to be the most effective, the CORE team *must* contain more than one person who can help develop others and who has the authority to lead collaborative efforts. This helps set the DNA of the entire organization.

When individual team members discover their purpose, and are working within their sweet spots, it gives a current leader the occasion to better see how each member might contribute to the leadership culture. This environment can develop a leadership team as team members begin to see their own leadership potential. The leadership team acts like the atom's electrons, balancing the positive charge in the nucleus through collaboration with the CORE team members. The leadership team eventually begins to operate as a leadership pipeline. People development becomes more than a conversation; it becomes the new reality that allows for organizational health and movement forward around clarity of vision and a determined purpose. My research demonstrates that the development of the CORE Team Leadership Model has the potential to move an organization beyond simply maintaining the status quo to a place of developing people who are working within their strengths for the common good of an organization.

I have always believed that we should take the best practices found within the business world and seek to implement these ideas within the ranks of our own leadership structure. Having worked at one of the largest semiconductor manufacturing companies in the United States, I saw firsthand many examples of solid leadership principles that I have incorporated in my own life. I have had the opportunity to meet savvy, strategic business thinkers who were always thinking outside the box and bringing their optima to the business world. One doesn't have to look far to see that the business world is continuing to grow in leadership development. I encourage you to learn from this model and build upon it within your organization.

7

COLLABORATION IN THE 21ST CENTURY WORKFORCE

"If everyone is moving forward together, then success takes care of itself."
—Henry Ford

In today's workforce the word "collaboration" is a buzzword, but do we understand the power of collaboration? Many organizations claim to have a collaborative work environment yet they lack evidence of this higher-level teamwork effort for accomplishing goals or creating something new. Collaboration only works if the leadership understands its value and is willing to allow their employs to achieve a common goal by sharing ideas and skills.

To foster a strong collaborative work environment, organizations must clearly define what collaboration looks like for them when looking at where they are as a company and where they want to go as they move forward. Companies must take seriously not only the differences within their teams but also how to leverage the strengths within their teams.

UNLOCKING A CULTURE OF COLLABORATION

It takes intentionality to promote a collaborative culture within your organization. Many organizations fail to create a collaborative workplace because they have not clearly defined the boundaries around collaboration. When employees are left to define the collaborative boundaries themselves without input from their leadership, they will usually align with the lowest common denominator of either the most talkative individual, the most power hungry in the group, or the one who has the largest interest in the project. Leaders who outline the boundaries will help ensure successful teamwork while mitigating these negative patterns.

A solid collaborative culture is one that understands the strengths and weaknesses of the organization and its team members. When you spend time working through the organizational strengths and weaknesses, you begin to see what your organization's

> It takes INTENTIONALITY to promote a collaborative culture within your organization.

unique status is within a given industry. For instance, if you are an energy company and you know that one of your strengths is your control of a large share of the market in the U.S., then you have a place to begin when it comes to building increased collaboration as you know where you stand with others in the same industry. Likewise, if you acknowledge that one of your weaknesses is working with other organizations, it allows you to put some strategic thought into how you might forge better working relationships to increase your collaborative efforts as your business grows.

Knowing your unique status also helps you ask the right questions. How do you currently solve problems in your organization? Is your company organized so that one or two people are your go-to problem solvers? Or is your culture organized around collaborative problem-solving? Answering these internal questions will help you gauge your collaboration margins and show the areas in which you need to start implementing a stronger collaborative mindset.

> *"Synergy without strategy results in a waste of energy."*
> *—Ogwo David Emenike*

As you move toward a more collaborative workplace, more team members will have the opportunity to operate from a place of strength as their roles become more clearly defined. Once people begin to see collaboration as an asset of your organization, collaboration can become a grassroots movement as leaders emerge from all levels of leadership and a collaborative culture can be firmly established.

Focusing primarily on leadership in his books, John C. Maxwell writes, "Becoming a leader is a lot like investing successfully in the stock market. If your hope is to make a fortune in a day, you're not going to be successful. What matters most is what you do day to day over the long haul." This day-to-day development of a collaborative culture helps train leaders to be collaborative and strengthens not only the team but also the organization as a whole. Maxwell goes on to say, "The secret of one's success is found in the daily agenda. If you continually invest in your leadership development, letting your assets compound, the inevitable result is growth over time."

When an organization is built upon collaboration and the leadership is committed to being collaborative, then collaboration moves from a chore to something that is desired as each member of the team grows and develops along the way. It is important to engage the right people in the collaborative process to make decisions as the organization moves forward. The individuals who are part of the team must have a voice and be invited not only to the discussion but also to facilitate the collaboration becoming a reality within the entire organization. Teams that value each participating member having weight in the discussion will develop over time a stronger vision and more in-depth leadership.

As leadership is developed at all levels of a company, one begins to realize that a firm plan must be in place to help each member grow from a mere spectator to one who owns the vision. The members within a collaborative team must continually guard collaboration from being hijacked and be willing to replace themselves for the sake of the entire organization if necessary.

GENERATIONAL SYNCHRONICITY

To understand collaboration among the generations, we must learn to embrace the differences each generation brings to the table through generational synchronicity. Generational synchronicity is the ability for multiple generations to recognize and respect the values unique to each generation, thus positively affecting their communication, productivity, and interpersonal relationships within the workplace. It's a strength-based look at collaboration versus focusing on and managing generational differences.

Companies that continue to develop and challenge multiple generations in the process of working together will see collaborative efforts rise. Collaboration increases through exploring what it would look like to be more intentional about intersections that merge generational lines. This desire to bridge generational gaps within the workplace is the basis for generational synchronicity. How does the leadership of your organization help foster relationships between employees of different generations? Does the leadership value input from all generations? Does your organization encourage the older employees to mentor the younger generations? How does your organization encourage older employees to take an active learning style from the younger generation?

To bridge generational gaps you must first begin reclaiming the word "generation." Most people think of a generation to mean a group of individuals living in a 20- to 30-year span; I now use it to describe a movement encompassing all persons alive on the earth at this time. Generational synchronicity, in essence, communicates a desire in which all age groups that are alive at this time to be a collective part of learning and developing together as they find ways to communicate with each other, learn from each other, and collaborate together to create a more positive working environment. Generational synchronicity increases the cohesion between team members which directly impacts the level of collaboration. Generational synchronicity is a necessary approach to developing legacy makers as it encourages leaders to build on the strengths that each generation brings to the workplace.

Questions to think about:

1. How does your organization define collaboration?

2. How collaborative is your organization?

3. How does your organization continue to foster a culture of collaboration?

4. In what ways can you build on the strengths of your multi-generational team?

5. How does generational synchronicity play out in your organization?

8
CLEARING MUDDY OBJECTIVES

"If you do not know where you are going, every road will get you nowhere."
—Henry A. Kissinger

Who are we and where are we going? It's amazing how many organizations cannot answer these questions. Every organization must be able to define the *vision* of who they are and the *mission* of where they are going. Everyone suffers when an organization lacks these clearly communicated objectives. Legacy makers help guide their organizations through the development of clear objectives of vision and mission with the prime target being its culture. The culture of your company keeps the vision and mission in focus and achievable over time.

I recently sat with a bright young leader who was thinking of leaving his job with a large company. As we talked he said, "I am not convinced this organization knows where it's going. It seems like we are in crisis, and I am not sure I trust the leadership to successfully navigate us to the next level." This uncertainty of a clear vision and mission left him struggling with his future in the company. This is becoming an all-too-common conversation that I have with people who are making the difficult decision to stay or exit an organization.

> One of the greatest disservices to our employees is not laying out for them a **CLEAR OBJECTIVE** of who we are and where we are going.

One of the greatest disservices to our employees is not laying out for them a clear objective of who we are and where we are going. Organizations that offer this clarity are cultivating the type of culture that raises up leaders and retains top talent.

AXIOLOGY—THE STUDY OF VALUE

I was recently exposed to the term that many within the business world have been privy to for some time now – *axiology*. In its simplest form, axiology is the study of value and of the kinds of things that are valuable. What a company values ultimately becomes the end result of an organization. The vision of an organization, if clearly stated, leads people to understand what that organization values and can help people see the results of a company's vision come to fruition within the daily, weekly, monthly, and yearly tasks.

To grasp the implications behind axiology and how it fits current leadership principles within the business world, one must delve deeper into the term to understand how this science of value came to be. Now deceased, Robert Hartman wrote, lectured, and taught on axiology for many years. According to Hartman, "Axiology as a science is the development of the definition of value in terms of the logical relation of the class membership: a thing has value in the degree in which it fulfills the concept of its class." In other words, what one values is revealed by what one does; what one does defines one's vision. A vision statement that sounds good but has nothing

> Conflicts often arise within organizations because of the lack of clarity over WHAT IS VALUED AND WHY.

to do with what one is actually doing is only there to check a box or impress others. A person, business, or organization reveals what they value by what they do, either substantiating or discrediting their visions; value plays an important role within today's organizations.

Conflicts often arise within organizations because of the lack of clarity over what is to be valued and why. Axiology seeks to understand three dimensions of value: systemic value, extrinsic value, and intrinsic value. Hartman uses the example of John, a young mathematics student, in the story below to illustrate each dimension:

> The best example for illustrating the interrelation of the three dimensions of value is love. Love is, of course, the value phenomenon par excellence. Let us take, as an example, a young mathematics student, John, who is going to Europe for his summer vacation. As he boards the Queen Elizabeth II, he says to himself,

"I am going to have myself a time!" In his mind is the image of a curve, undulating, which belongs to the concept "girl." At that moment, this is nothing but a systemic concept; for he is thinking of no girl in particular but only of what might be called the principle of femininity. The second day out there is a dance and, as is customary on European boats, the girls are lined up on one side of the hall and the young men on the other. As he stares at the young ladies opposite, his valuation changes from systemic to extrinsic.

Now he is seeing real girls, examples of the class "girl," from whom the common properties of the concept "girl" have been abstracted. His extrinsic valuation consists in applying the yardstick of this concept, "girl," to the examples of girlhood before him, to see which one of them fulfills this concept to the greatest degree, that is, which one has the greatest number of the properties of "girl." He weighs, as it were —and it is interesting to note that the Greek word axios is the English axle, meaning the axle of a scale — he weighs, as it were, the girls against their own girl-measure, namely, "girl." He finally decides on one of the girls and dances with her. While they dance, the same process of extrinsic valuation continues; he compares what he has in his arms with what he has in his mind. He dances with a few other girls and finally decides that one of them, Betty, is the best girl, which does not mean that she is morally the best but rather that, to the greatest degree, she fulfills the properties in question. He has a glorious voyage.

But the day before the ship is due to arrive at Southampton, something happens to him which seems utterly irrational and can only be explained by formal axiology. When he awakens in the morning, a thought suddenly takes hold of him: Betty is not just a girl, a member of the class of girls who can be compared to other girls, but she is the only girl in the world and incomparable! He knows full well that there are one thousand million girls in the world, yet, he knows with equal certainty, and actually with greater certainty, that Betty is the only girl in the world. From this he logically concludes that, since he is a man and a man cannot live without a woman, and since she is the only woman in the world, he must live with her. He writes her an extremely strange letter, filled with poetic words and such metaphors as "my treasure," "my incomparable one," telling her that she must marry him and, adding in a postscript, that if she doesn't he will throw himself overboard. All this from a mathematician.

Hartman does a brilliant job of explaining how the process moves from a systemic valuation to extrinsic value to intrinsic value found in the concept of love. What does love and axiology have to do with business and the development of leader? Everything. When teams do not have a solid understanding of what they truly value, things begin to slowly go off-kilter. Having a grasp of axiology, therefore, is vitally important for the grounding of a team within an organization.

In 2012, I had the opportunity to interview Whit Mitchell via teleconference. Mitchell is the president and CEO of Working In-Sync, an organization that specializes in stepping into companies and helping people in leadership positions understand behavioral management and axiology. Mitchell got his start understanding teams, team dynamics, and team management while working as a rowing coach at Dartmouth College in Hanover, New Hampshire. He began to see how teams function in tandem when the objectives are clear and the systems are in place for success.

This understanding of teams led him to an opportunity to work with high-caliber athletes and Olympic athletes in customizing their training regiments and instructing them on strategies to calm themselves in the midst of competition. Eventually, Mitchell began working with different corporate CEOs in the workplace. One of his clients was the Boston Bruins of the National Hockey League, who won the 2011 Stanley Cup. He spent time helping them understand how to value working together as a team as well as working as individuals. One would think that understanding the value of teamwork would be automatic for competitors such as athletes within the NHL. Mitchell had

> *"Vision without action is merely a dream. Action without vision just passes the time. Vision with action can change the world."*
> —*Joel A. Barker*

them think about what the team valued and the nature of competition. Did his influence and coaching have anything to do with their Stanley Cup win? One never knows for sure; however, it may have played a vital role to their successful season.

Mitchell helped me understand the study of value within a business set-ting by challenging me with my own clarity of vision. Mitchell says that the importance of vision in conjunction with value is what many people do not grasp. Mitchell warns that the "lack of clarity is oftentimes at the heart of [their difficulties] of a majority of the cliental I work with. Help-ing them clearly articulate what they value in a way that everyone within the company understands, can speak about, and buy into is a large part of my time spent working with corporations." During the interview, I was reminded that what one *values* is what one *produces*. When what one val-ues becomes muddled or preoccupied with too many things, one loses the ability to clearly articulate vision to a team; once the desired goals are clarified, vision comes to fruition.

As one continues to study value and how it fits into clear objectives, it be-comes apparent that axiology must be applied to the initial development of organizations for success within the team. Without a clear understand-ing of what the team values, it becomes difficult to know how to formu-late team members according to their sweet spots. The more the team understands what it values, the more clearly it can cast a vision within all levels of leadership. Vision comes after values are defined not vice versa. A vision statement written solely from a two day, off-site training program will only be words on a page unless the team has already been practicing the training's principles, therefore, substantiating their value.

In his book *Empowered Leaders*, Hans Finzel alludes to a leader's respon-sibility in this process of clearly understanding how to communicate the values of an organization. Finzel uses Lou Holtz, retired football coach of Notre Dame, as an example:

> After taking the team to one hundred wins in his eleven-year tenure, he says the biggest problem in trying to lead today is everyone is talking about rights and privileges whereas twenty-five years ago people talked about obligations and responsibilities. Yet he adjusted his coaching style to deal successfully with a new mindset and thus led his team to one victory after another.

Holtz understood that for the team to function effectively, the leader must consistently keep what is valuable in front of the team members.

For a healthy organization to exist and function at the highest level possible, the values that are the most important must rise to the surface. These values must be discovered through discussions, assessments, and seeking to understand the culture of the team and the culture in which the team is working. The organization's vision is revealed by what is valued and is tested in the day-to-day operations of the organization. As the vision is defined, the organization must consistently strive for clarity of vision, asking itself if what it values matches the results it is achieving. Periodically asking this question continues to keep the organization focused on the values that hold the vision in place.

> "If you are working on something exciting that you really care about, you don't have to be pushed. The vision pulls you."
> —Steve Jobs

Leaders who desire to leave behind a legacy continue to ask themselves questions: "Do my values translate to the personal lives of the team I lead? Do my values keep me awake at night when I see the collision of what my organization believes and what I believe? Do I promote what I say I believe even when I am off the clock?" Once values have affected every area of life, then clarity around the objectives has occurred. This leads to complete sticking power.

Questions to think about:

1. What is your organization's objective?

2. What are you aiming at? (Vision)

3. How does that objective line up with your company's values? And your personal values?

4. How clear is your objective to all employees at every level of your organization?

5. How will you accomplish this objective? (Mission)

9
RAISING UP LEADERS UPON LEADERS

"Growing other leaders from the ranks
isn't just the duty of the leader, it's an obligation."
—Warren Bennis

RAISING UP YOUR REPLACEMENT

Are you raising up your replacement yet? Many times, when I ask this question I get blank stares, deafening silence, and some uneasy squirming. My favorite response to this question came from a CEO of a large company who said with complete confidence, "Yes, I have identified my replacement. I have the names of three people who could replace me written on a 3x5 card in the top drawer of my desk."

"Have you told them this?"

He responded, "No. My secretary and the president of the board know where to find that card should something happen to me."

"That is not raising up leaders," I said. "That is leadership by abdication. Yes, the company has a choice of three candidates to replace you; however, names written on a 3x5 card is not a succession plan nor is it sound leadership." My response was not well received.

Succession planning is hard work. It's not done overnight. It takes knowing the culture and overall health of an organization and its employees as well as the ongoing needs within that organization. It also takes knowing the strengths and weaknesses of your team members and being aware of what they need to continue to move forward. Most organizations do not spend enough time on succession planning and it shows. According to the American Management Association, its takes between six weeks to three months to fill most vacant jobs in today's organizations. This is due in large part to a lack of leadership development and succession planning.

> Succession planning is HARD WORK. It's not done overnight.

Succession planning is nothing more than preparing your team for the next level. It's knowing the state of your team and putting a performance plan in place so they can continue to develop in their careers. Too often we allow the "next man up" mentality to be good enough. The "next man up" mentality dictates that whoever is next in line or whoever has the longest track record will be the next person to be promoted. This unfortunately is not succession planning. Rather this is hoping that the next person in line has somehow learned what is required to do the job. True succession planning happens when leaders think through the specific steps they will take to raise up employees within their organizations.

Legacy makers are those who put the time in to learn how to raise up leaders. When working with leaders, I take them through the process of developing a collaborative culture and defining clear objectives. We then discuss how they currently raise up leaders within their organizations and determine if a more concise process for developing leaders in needed. A clear roadmap for leadership development is important both for the organization and for the individual employee. Clarity provides stability for employees which in turn promotes their sense of ownership and commitment to the company.

THREE KINDS OF STARS

Every organization has them and in fact, you can probably place yourself in one of these categories. Three types of high performers are constantly shining among us in our organizations: the rock stars, the superstars, and the shooting stars. I was first introduced to this concept in the book *The Everyone Culture: Becoming a Deliberately Developmental Organization*. What is interesting about each of the high performers is that they are seen within all generations from the Silent Generation to Generation Z. Learning how to embrace them, how to harness them, and how to develop them will give your organization the competitive advantage when it comes to building a legacy that lasts.

Rock Stars

These are the people within your organization that are steady, hard-working, and overall committed to the company. They care about the company, like their jobs, and will find ways to push the company forward with their contributions. These people are rock solid employees. They are content to work and grow with a company as long as they are treated fairly and their contributions are acknowledged.

It is important to give rock stars the opportunity to develop their skills and knowledge base by giving them room to spread their wings and to experience all that the company has to offer. Rock stars can often be overlooked because they don't rock the boat. Though they are high performers, they do not seek attention or the limelight. They want to be recognized for their individual contributions but are just as satisfied when the team succeeds.

Leading a rock star is easy. They are self-motivated and will look for opportunities to develop themselves both personally and professionally. Continue giving them support and encouragement as you help them see how they fit into the vision of your organization.

Superstars

Superstars are individuals who also like their jobs and have a desire to grow and develop. They look toward future possibilities and believe that they can contribute to the heartbeat of an organization. They are content to stay at an organization but are highly driven by their desire to advance. If advancement within a company does not happen in a timely manner, they will look for advancement opportunities outside the organization.

When you recognize a superstar, find ways to give them opportunities to shine. They like to work on projects that are challenging because they know this will give them the tools necessary for promotions. Because superstars are driven, they will continue to hone their skills to achieve a competitive edge. They will be committed to a company as long as you reassure them that the prospect for advancement is in place.

Leading superstars takes a little finesse as they tend to see a pretty clear picture of their future and are constantly looking for ways to get to the next phase of their career. When working with these individuals, allow them to gain independence as their knowledge of their job increases and give them the authority to make decisions. They will meet the goals you set for them with less supervision and more positive feedback.

Shooting Stars

The top level of high performers are the shooting stars. These individuals enter a company and quickly rise within the organization. They may even be your boss someday. These high-performing individuals are well adept at seeing and plugging into the big picture. They are passionate, cool under pressure, and are fearless decision-makers.

When managing a shooting star, the sky is the limit for what they can accomplish for your organization. Seek to harness their energy and ambition by outlining clear expectations and well-defined performance guidelines. Keeping their job interesting gives them the chance to shine even when there are limited advancement opportunities. They will be amazing leaders, and your organization's culture will benefit from their confidence and expertise.

Less is more when leading a shooting star. Be mindful of keeping them continually challenged and maintaining loose reins. The more you understand their need to excel, the longer they will be an asset to your organization. As soon as the challenge is over or they decide to move onto something else, it is difficult to keep them engaged.

KNOWING THE STATE OF YOUR ORGANIZATION

The first stage of raising up leaders is knowing the current state of your organization. How are people promoted within your company? What requirements are expected of them? How are those requirements communicated? Many organizations

> "The greatest leader is not necessarily the one who does the greatest things. He is the one that gets the people to do the greatest things."
> —Ronald Reagan

have an outline for growth; however, it is often buried somewhere on their website or deep within the human resources department's filing system. Knowing your organization is about assessing the health of your organization and its teams. In his book *Pushing Back Entropy: Moving Teams from Conflict to Health*, author Andy Johnson helps us understand what makes a healthy team. In the prologue to his book, Johnson describes the premise of his book this way: "Sliding toward conflict is natural, and moving away from conflict towards healthy team development requires sustained energy and focus." Johnson offers specific questions to guide you in assessing the health of your organization as a whole and to give you valuable insight into the health of your team(s):

1. What are the characteristics of a healthy team?
2. How do you create shared character?
3. What does it mean to operate with laser clarity?
4. What are the communication barriers within your organization?

These and many other questions are addressed within his work on teams. I would highly recommend reading Andy Johnson's book. You will never raise up employees in a healthy way until you know the environment in which those employees are operating.

It is important to think through job descriptions as you assess the health of your organization. Your employees experience greater job satisfaction when their job responsibilities and work methods are spelled out for them. You may be surprised how often someone is hired with an outdated job description and are left floundering to figure out how to complete the job that is in front of them. Job benchmarking is a method that helps prevent this from happening. Job

> "A leader takes people where they want to go. A great leader takes people where they don't necessarily want to go, but ought to be."
> —Rosalynn Carter

benchmarking allows the job to speak for itself. This process allows an organization to look at each role and ask questions to pin down precisely what is required to achieve superior job performance. From the requirements, a job description is created that helps assure clarity around what the job is asking of an employee. You can even go a step further and have employees take an assessment that you can overlay with the job benchmark to ensure fit and long-term job satisfaction. Price Associates are some of the best facilitators I have worked with in regard to job benchmarking. (See Price Associates' website at price-associates.com for more information on job benchmarking.)

KNOWING THE STATE OF YOUR EMPLOYEES

Once you have assessed the health of your organization, the next step is knowing the state of your employees. What do your employees need to continue to grow? Where are they on their growth and development trajectory? Knowing where each individual employee is in their personal development allows you to plan and implement subsequent steps for their continued growth. You cannot raise up employees unless you truly know them. You cannot put together a growth plan in a vacuum; you must assess them with their input. The best employee development plans are designed for the employee to lead the conversation. Most employees know where they need to grow; we just rarely invite them into the conversation.

Fig. 1.2

THE CORE TALENT MATRIX

When I first started working with organizations around the topic of talent management and raising up the next generation of leaders, I adapted the nine-box matrix from the Association for Talent Management. I named my adaptation the CORE Talent Matrix and used it as a way of helping leaders assess their teams and employees (see Figure 1.2). Most commonly used in succession planning, this matrix can help you identify potential leaders within your organization. However, after several attempts to use this matrix personally among some of the leadership networks I was working with, I realized it lacked depth and objectivity. I then began to focus on individualized growth plans and the identification of roles. I now only reference the CORE Talent Matrix to enhance the conversation around potential and productivity when discussing the CORE Team Leadership Model.

While there is some merit to the CORE Talent Matrix, it falls short in several areas. The primary issue with this matrix is that it is too subjective in nature. This subjective approach to leadership development is dangerous and does not take into account several factors when assessing an employee: the required skill set for the job, the employee's level of self-awareness, the existence of a clear path for personal and professional development, and the company's ability to train its employees for success. As leaders, we can and do move people into jobs that they never had the skills to excel in. Leaders must take responsibility for knowing the state of their employees and the skill level necessary for their success before raising them up and promoting them to the next level.

Another area this matrix breaks down is in job fit. We can rank someone along the matrix only to find that the job in which we are moving them toward is not the right fit. Or perhaps we have promoted someone into a job that is no longer the right fit. Or we may promote someone into a new role that is outside of their skill set. I worked with one leader who raised up and promoted an employee to a management position because he was good at his job, but he had never actually led anyone. It wasn't long before this employee left the company feeling defeated. Was the breakdown the promoted employee's fault? Or was it the fault of the leader who promoted the employee out of his skill set? Although the employee had the responsibility to speak up when feeling overwhelmed with the leadership requirements, the greater onus was on the leader who promoted the employee without knowing if his employee fit the job.

If we are going to promote employees within our organizations, we must think about leadership development from a deeper level. We must identify the leadership gaps within our organizations. Leadership gaps include but are not limited to: skilled workers, critical thinking, self-awareness, changes to industry standards, the use of technology, new technology, and shifting leadership structures. Once you identify the leadership gap or gaps, you then must find ways to ensure that you are raising up the right people for the right jobs. That responsibility falls squarely on the leader and one that has dire consequences should the leader decide to shirk this responsibility.

THE LEADERSHIP GAP

It is important to understand the current percentage of each generation within the workforce. Figure 1.3 is an original compilation of my research. The year 2018

By 2028, 61% OF THE WORKFORCE will consist of the Millennial Generation and Generation Z.

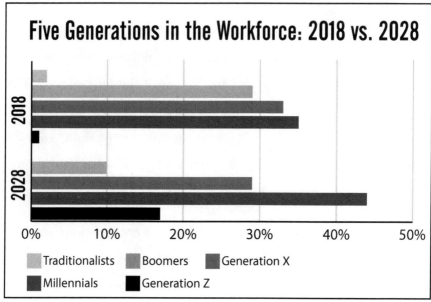

Fig. 1.3

marks the true turning point where the power is shifting to a younger generation. Though it's not a massive shift at this time, within the next ten years that gap will continue to grow. By 2028, 61% of the workforce will consist of the Millennial Generation and Generation Z. This statistic reveals to us the need to think differently about how we raise up and promote individuals within our organizations.

Understanding and accepting that the workforce is getting younger and that employees are going to need greater leadership development allows for organizations to begin to think now about the role of leadership development programs. It is crucial to have a robust leadership development program in place that gives your employees the opportunity to develop both interpersonal skills as well as the skills to lead others. This provides your organization with a competitive advantage when it comes to retention and long-term success as you pivot to meet the changing face of this new younger workforce. Remember, this younger workforce is not only coming into the job market; they are also coming into leadership positions within our organizations and will lead differently than their traditionalist and baby boomer counterparts. The landscape is changing on many different fronts.

Knowing your employees means knowing what they need to grow and develop. Creating an individualized growth plan for their success helps ensure that each employee has every advantage to move up within your organization and helps them see the pathway to achievement. After all, it's about raising up employees and eventually finding your replacement.

IDENTIFY THE NEXT ROLE

What's next for you and the people who serve under you and with you? Have you sat down and talked with them about where they want to go next? Have you had the conversation about the steps necessary to acquire the skills and competencies to be ready for the next level within your organization? Many employees are not ready for the next level because they have not identified what their next role is. Some only know their next role because they have learned the hierarchical leadership model and have settled into waiting for their opportunity to be promoted upon the position being vacated. Ideally, an employee's boss is part of the conversation in addressing subsequent roles. Leaders need to help their employees think through how to move on or up; both are important conversations.

Simply sitting down and addressing the fact that most succession plans are assumed and not spelled out helps us bridge the gap between generations. I recently had a conversation with a younger employee who asked me what steps she could take to uncover her next role at her company. She had been assuming for some time that her next promotion would be to fill her boss's job. She inquired about her options since her company was not taking any forward steps to make that happen.

> Simply sitting down and addressing the fact that MOST SUCCESSION PLANS ARE ASSUMED and not spelled out helps us bridge the gap between generations.

As we talked, I challenged her to sit down and have the conversation with her boss to explore her options for a new role. With her permission, I also challenged her boss to reach out to this employee. Both leaders and employees can benefit from keeping track of their conversations via written communication, cloud-based storage or audio recording devices. This strategy helps ensure the conversation is not simply a one-time occurrence but one that initiates a growth plan, including goals and a prospective timeline.

To bridge the leadership gap and be successful within the next ten years, you must be intentional about raising up employees and finding ways to connect them to your organization's vision and values. When your employees see that they are valuable to your organization, the easier it will be for them to make the leap into owning their roles and viewing your company as a home rather than a place to collect a paycheck.

By 2028, the majority of employees in the workforce will be viewing their jobs differently than those workers currently employed. You can begin to bridge this future leadership gap by connecting the dots between job expectations and job significance. My friend Gabrielle Bosché is the founder of The Millennial Solution, a training and resource group that works with organizations around the topic of retention of top millennial talent. Gabrielle has determined that mismanaged expectations drive much of a company's failure to retain employees. You must have clear expectations of what a prospective employee can anticipate when working at your

> By 2028, the majority of employees in the workforce will be VIEWING THEIR JOBS DIFFERENTLY than those workers currently employed.

company and a compelling context as to why your company exists. Inspiring and motivating even your youngest employees through well-defined expectations and the whys that drive your company puts you further ahead of many companies I work with when it comes to bridging the leadership gap. (For more information on The Millennial Solution training opportunities and additional resources, see millennialsolution.com.)

INDIVIDUALIZED GROWTH PLANS

As the generational shift continues within our organizations, the need to create individualized growth plans intensifies. There is no one-size-fits-all solution when it comes to leadership development. Nothing can substitute sitting down with an employee and helping them assess their current growth areas and to outline what it's going to take them to gain the competitive edge for their next promotion.

As you think through individualized growth plans, consider these questions to guide the development of a plan that will benefit both you and your employee: What assessments can I use to measure this employee's strengths and weaknesses? What specific area is this employee wanting to work on? What is their motivation level? Am I telling them they have to grow? I have worked with people from both sides of individualized growth plans. One young man I worked with was told by his organization that he needed to work through a growth plan put in place by his company or else he was no longer going to be employed. I knew within the first few minutes of our coaching session that this growth plan was not something that he wanted to do. Although our coaching time was cordial, it wasn't long before he found another job and left the organization.

I have also worked with individuals who sought out a growth plan because they knew the only way to get to the next level within their personal and professional development was to cultivate a plan. They went looking for and actively implemented the tools from our conversations. They experienced great success in their careers and moved into leadership positions by taking a posture of learning and by following a growth plan focused on advancement opportunities. In addition, mentoring is a key part of a healthy growth plan and can bring about true and lasting change as you address the ever-widening leadership gap. (See "The Boomer Message" for more on mentoring and its benefits.)

USING A READINESS INDICATOR

Once you have assessed your employees through identifying their next roles and generating individualized growth plans, you can use a readiness indicator to help you determine whether they are ready to move into a new role. Below is an example of a readiness indicator:

Red. This employee is not ready for the next role. They have either not identified a growth plan or have not been working on the plan that has been put in place. Further conversations with this employee may result in either moving them to yellow or exiting the organization.

Yellow. This employee is currently working on the identified growth plan and is progressing at a healthy pace; however, they are not ready for the next role. Keep in mind that this level isn't negative. Rather, it helps you guard against promoting a team member too quickly which can short-circuit their growth and development.

Green. This employee is ready for the next role and needs to be reassessed using the process of identifying the next step and setting up a growth plan. Depending on the information from those conversations, this employee may benefit from a new challenge or is ready to be raised up to the next level within the organization. Your job as a leader is to help identify the next right step.

This process can be laborious and can get lost in the list of things that have to be done within your organization. Organizations that take time to assess their organizational and employee health are the companies that retain employees. When organizations create pathways to raise up employees, they are embracing a culture of leadership development and are getting to the CORE of what's next for the organization. Pat yourself on the back if you have gotten this far in the process because the next step is launching those employees to make positive and lasting changes for the organization far beyond your reach.

Questions to think about:

1. How does your organization currently raise up leaders?

2. How important is professional development within your organization?

3. Do your employees know their next steps for growth?

4. Have you assessed the health of your organization? How healthy is your organization?

5. Have you assessed your team members using any of the information from this chapter? What were the results?

10
EMPOWERING YOUR TEAM

"As we look ahead into the next century,
leaders will be those who empower others."
—Bill Gates

Empowerment is the final element of the CORE Team Leadership Model for inspiring solid leadership development within organizations. The ability to raise up employees and to allow them to do meaningful work is a difficult skill to learn as a leader. It is easy to delegate meaningless tasks or busy work to employees. As my friend Corey Sanford says, "We should look at delegation as one of the most meaningful leadership development tools at our disposal." Legacy makers use delegation not only to entrust employees with tasks and responsibilities but also to empower them to achieve all they can for the company. These leaders understand that employee development is not just about controlling the organization; it needs to allow the organization to breathe within a culture of empowered leaders empowering others.

L. David Marquet wrote one of the greatest books I have read on this process of empowering teams. In his book *Turn the Ship Around*, Marquet talks about how as a captain he helped shape a culture of leaders who were empowered to make decisions. His journey of taking one of the Navy's lowest performing submarines and turning it into the best functioning submarine illustrates what can happen when a leader moves from standard take-control authority to give-control empowerment. Leaders struggle with empowering others for a myriad of reasons. For some it's fear that someone will do it better. For others it's fear of losing control and facing consequences of what might happen then. For others it's simply a lack of trust in their employees to accomplish the task.

Embracing a culture of empowerment is challenging; however, empowerment is about releasing power that allows team members within your organization the opportunity to grow and develop. I tell leaders at this point to expect it will get messy because relationships with people are messy; so be prepared for the mess. Some of the greatest leadership lessons that employees will ever learn will be in cleaning up messes. I know this from experience. Leadership development is about celebrating the good and learning from the bad. Both help shape us to become valuable team members.

To demonstrate empowered organizations, I want to introduce two organizations that have led the way in empowering employees. We will examine Mars, Incorporated and Gore Technology. Both of these companies have made employee empowerment an important part of their corporate environment. I will briefly share their stories and how each of their leadership models have challenged the status quo. I then extrapolate from my observations what can be gleaned from both companies and the transferrable principles that can be incorporated into the development of empowering teams within organizations.

MARS, INCORPORATED

In 1911 in Tacoma, Washington, Frank C. Mars made his first candies in his kitchen. These initial candies established the groundwork for Frank's soon-to-be confectionery company.

> In the 1920s, Forrest E. Mars, Sr. joined his father in business and together they launched the MILKY WAY® bar. In 1932, Forrest, Sr. moved to the United Kingdom with a dream of building a business based on the philosophy of a "mutuality of benefits" for all stakeholders – this vision serves as the foundation of the Mars, Incorporated a diverse global business that employees 65,000 associates in 71 countries.

As Mars continued to grow, it began to diversify from simply sweets to many other products, such as pet foods, chewing gum, drinks, and now even into science and research. The subset companies represented under the Mars, Incorporated banner are thinking creatively when it comes to empowerment and leadership. Mars, In-

> "Leadership is unlocking people's potential to become better."
> —Bill Bradley

corporated has five guiding values that govern everything it does: Quality, Responsibility, Mutuality, Efficiency, and Freedom. These five values can be found in both its corporate dealings and its leadership structure.

Quality

The understanding of empowerment and quality begins with how the associates of Mars, Incorporated function with one another and how they interact on a day-to-day basis. Each individual understands the importance of their personal quality as a way being empowered to own their portion of the job:

> Our company is dedicated to the highest quality in all the work we do. Quality is the uncompromising standard for our actions, and it flows from our passion and our pride in being part of the Mars community. Quality work, which results from our personal efforts, is the first ingredient of quality brands and the source of our reputation for high standards.

Responsibility

The empowering for taking on direct responsibility allows the associates of Mars, Incorporated to make and to own their decisions and take action when needed, without having to go through large amounts of red tape in the process:

> We choose to be different from those corporations where many levels of management dilute personal responsibility. All associates are asked to take direct responsibility for results, to ex-

ercise initiative and judgment and to make decisions as required. By recruiting ethical people well suited to their jobs and trusting them, we ask associates to be accountable for their own high standards.

Mutuality

Mars, Incorporated empowers the individual and believes in people above product. When the people within the team are more important than the outcomes of the team, it encourages the associates to respond by working hard and seeking the best for the company:

> *We believe the standard by which our business relationships should be measured is the degree to which mutual benefits are created. These benefits can take many different forms, and need not be strictly financial in nature. Likewise, while we must try to achieve the most competitive terms, the actions of Mars should never be at the expense, economic or otherwise, of others with whom we work.*

Efficiency

Because Mars, Incorporated places high value on its people and on teams over hierarchical structure, its business runs efficiently and quite lean. This empowering of people allows both the associates and the company to benefit equally from its efficient use of resources:

> *How is it possible to maintain our principles, offering superior value for money and sharing our success? Our strength lies in*

our efficiency, the ability to organize all our assets – physical, fi-
nancial and human – for maximum productivity. In this way, our
products and services are made and delivered with the highest
quality, at the least possible cost, with the lowest consumption
of resources; similarly, we seek to manage all our business opera-
tions with the most efficient processes for decision making.

Freedom

Creative thinking and placing high value on being free and unrestricted as a company allows Mars, Incorporated the ability to continue to empower its people over financial profit:

We need freedom to shape our future; we need profit to remain
free. Mars is one of the world's largest family-owned corpora-
tions. This family ownership is a deliberate choice. Many com-
panies began as Mars did, but as they grew larger and required
new sources of funds, they sold stocks or incurred restrictive debt
to fuel their business. To extend their growth, they exchanged a
portion of their freedom. We believe growth and prosperity can
be achieved another way.

This philosophy brings freedom for all involved within the company and gives Mars, Incorporated the ability to continue to explore how empowerment can make a difference in the lives of its associates and the corporation as whole. Mars, Incorporated demonstrates the value of empowerment and puts into practice how empowering employees can be implemented within a company's culture, creating an environment benefitting all involved:

> The five principles of Quality, Responsibility, Mutuality, Efficiency and Freedom are the foundation of our culture and our approach to business. They unite us across generations, geographies, languages and cultures. Our Five Principles are synonymous with Mars and have been guiding Mars associates throughout most of our company's history. Every day, we do our best to put our principles into action through our work and our relationships with our consumers, customers, business partners, communities and one another.

These five principles show the importance of empowering employees through open dialogue between leaders and employees. This dialogue, however, must move beyond simply talking about the *value* of empowerment and move into *ownership and implementation* of empowerment within all areas of leadership. It is important to learn to engage with successful businesses within the world that are thinking outside the box in building an employee-empowering culture and challenging the traditional corporate hierarchical leadership many companies have used for years.

GORE TECHNOLOGIES

What happens when a company decides from the beginning that people are more important than technology? Gore Tech. What happens when a company promotes creativity in the midst of cutting-edge technology?

Gore Tech. What happens when a company says to its employees that one can own his or her own destiny within one's company? Gore Tech. From its inception, Gore Tech has been about innovation and releasing the employee to succeed and fly high in the midst of the

> *"The organization is, above all, social. It is people."*
> *—Peter Drucker*

cutthroat technology market in which it finds itself. Gore Tech is a leading innovator and thinker in the technology field, yet it has made a decision to value empowerment above product:

> *Founded in 1958, W. L. Gore & Associates, Inc. is a privately-held company headquartered in Newark, Delaware, USA. For more than 50 years, Gore has built a worldwide reputation for ethics and integrity in its dealings with customers, suppliers, and employees, and for taking a long-term view when assessing business situations. Today, Gore has more than 9,500 employees, called associates, located in 30 countries, with manufacturing facilities in the United States, Germany, United Kingdom, Japan and China, and sales offices around the world.*

> *Annual revenues are $3 billion. Our fluoropolymer products provide innovative solutions throughout industry, in next-generation electronics, for medical products, and with high-performance fabrics. We've repeatedly been named among the "100 Best Companies to Work For," in the U.S. by FORTUNE magazine, and our culture is a model for contemporary organizations seek-*

ing growth by unleashing creativity and fostering teamwork.

While we may be best known for our GORE-TEX® fabrics, all our products are distinguished in their markets. Our technologies and fluoropolymer expertise are unsurpassed. We create next-generation cable assemblies and components for the electronics industry, set the standard for outerwear comfort and protection, solve difficult industrial problems with innovative materials and technology, and Gore medical products work in harmony with the body's own tissues to restore normal body function.

We take our reputation for product leadership seriously, continually delivering new products and better solutions to the marketplaces of the world.

Gore Tech believes that when a working environment is healthy, people function at a higher level and the entire company benefits from their empowerment. This enhances a healthy culture within the workplace. Gore Tech defines its culture by its emphasis on its people:

How we work at Gore Tech sets us apart. Since Bill Gore founded the company in 1958, Gore Tech has been a team-based, flat lattice organization that fosters personal initiative. There are no traditional organizational charts, no chains of command, nor predetermined channels of communication. Instead, we communicate directly with each other and are accountable to fellow members of our multi-disciplined teams. We encourage hands-on innovation, involving those closest to a project in decision-making. Teams organize around opportunities and leaders emerge. This unique kind of corporate structure has proven to be a significant contributor to associate satisfaction and retention.

Gore Tech continues to explain how this culture is expressed within its corporation on a day-to-day basis:

We work hard at maximizing individual potential, maintaining an emphasis on product integrity, and cultivating an environment where creativity can flourish. A fundamental belief in our people and their abilities continues to be the key to our success. How does all this happen? Associates (not employees) are hired for general work areas. With the guidance of their sponsors (not bosses) and a growing understanding of opportunities and team objectives, associates commit to projects that match their skills. All of this takes place in an environment that combines freedom with cooperation and autonomy with synergy.

Everyone can earn the credibility to define and drive projects. Sponsors help associates chart a course in the organization that will offer personal fulfillment while maximizing their contribution to the enterprise. Leaders may be appointed, but are defined by "followership." More often, leaders emerge naturally by demonstrating special knowledge, skill, or experience that advances a business objective.

This ability to own the direction of one's team while moving away from hierarchical leadership gives the team the ability to be innovative and empowers people to function within their sweets spots.

Gore Tech has four basic guiding principles articulated by Bill Gore that helps motivate and facilitate its people to discover their niches:

> *Fairness to each other and everyone with whom we come in contact; freedom to encourage, help, and allow other associates to grow in knowledge, skill, and scope of responsibility; the ability to make one's own commitments and keep them; and consultation with other associates before undertaking actions that could impact the reputation of the company.*

Gore Tech has thought through the importance of empowerment within its company and how these values are lived out daily. Once again, the standard corporate hierarchy of boss and employees is replaced with a leadership team made up of associates all working together and empowered to find their sweet spots through innovative thinking. Leaders rise up naturally due to their strengths that all associates embrace. The associates themselves are allowed to be creative and own the direction of the company's vision with their values becoming the end result of the company as it moves forward.

There are many ways to enable team members to find their sweet spots via books, articles and online tests. Target Training International (TTI), an innovative leader in research-based behavioral assessment tools, has designed several products that are helpful in discovering people's distinctive strengths and skill sets. The TTI Success Insights® DISC assessment is particularly useful. DISC stands for dominance, influence, steadiness and compliance. This assessment identifies a person's dominant personality traits. It helps others on the team understand each team member's personality and how to better interact with them. Additionally, TTI 12 Driving Forces® (Motivators) assessment provides each participant with their four primary driving forces, four situational driving forces, and four indifferent driving forces. I have seen this assessment be instrumental in not only empowering employees but allowing employees to grow and develop within their organizations.

The assessment I have found to be the most comprehensive is the TTI Talent Insights® assessment. TTI's website offers a compelling description of this product:

> Combining both behaviors (DISC) and 12 Driving Forces (Motivators) into one integrated report, Talent Insights explains the how *and* why *behind a person's actions. Understand behaviors individuals bring to a team while uncovering motivators behind those behaviors. Get to know individual employees or capture a snapshot of the entire team with this innovative report.*
>
> **Commonly used to:** *engage employees, coach leaders, build better communication and to select the right team members for the right positions.*

If given the freedom to grow and develop in their sweet spots, team members gain the necessary skills to be empowered employees and to live out their callings and passions to the success of their organizations.

THE TIPPING POINT

During the early stages of my research, I discovered a tipping point within organizations that eventually moved an organization to the next level. This tipping point consists of a series of three elements: empower, promote, and launch. When an organization focuses on these elements with its employees, a more significant change begins to happen:

> *"Businesses often forget about the culture, and ultimately, they suffer for it because you can't deliver good service from unhappy employees."*
> —Tony Hsieh, Zappos

they are able to raise up new leaders from within.

At what point does an organization start to see a culture of leadership development emerge? What is the momentum builder that triggers a shift from simply talking about a leadership culture to having an actual leadership culture? The momentum builder is team empowerment.

Questions to think about:

1. Are team members empowered within your organization?
2. In what ways does your organization empower its employees?
3. In what ways does your organization disempower its employees?
4. Have you identified your replacement?

5. In what ways are you proactively empowering your replacement to do your job?

11
COMMITTING TO THE PROCESS

"The three great essentials to achieve anything worthwhile are, first, hard work; second, stick-to-itiveness; third, common sense."
—*Thomas Edison*

N othing of value happens without hard work. If you have made it this far, you have thought through some difficult concepts around generational strengths and weaknesses. You have looked at a model for developing leaders and have considered what is next for your organization. Now let's tie this process together by examining how you can achieve generational synchronicity within your organization while developing leaders using the CORE Team Leadership Model. Knowing how each generation responds to each part of the leadership model is instrumental in the process of empowering, promoting, and launching leaders within your organization.

COLLABORATION IN THE WORKPLACE

When fostering a more collaborative workplace and finding ways to work together multi-generationally, it is vital for a leader to know that effective collaboration will look differently for each generation.

> *"It takes a deep commitment to change and an even deeper commitment to grow."*
> —*Ralph Ellison*

TRADITIONALISTS/BABY BOOMERS: Both traditionalists and baby boomers see the importance of collaboration but will not often initiate it on their own. They will generally wait to be instructed to collaborate by leadership. These two generations can be highly collaborative by nature; however, they fear that giving away too much information may lead to no longer being needed. This fear may make them hesitant to collaborate.

GENERATION X: Gen Xers may initially be suspect of collaboration in the workplace. They will begin to collaborate with friends before they will collaborate with acquaintances or other people with whom they do not have regular interaction. Over time they see the power of collaboration and will actually fully engage in the process.

MILLENNIALS: Employees from the Millennial Generation have been waiting for collaboration in the workplace. They want to engage because it is through collaboration that they learn. They like the give-and-take of ideas and mental sparring that takes place through collaboration. Collaboration is something that many millennials expect in their workplace and are concerned when it doesn't happen.

GENERATION Z: Right out of the gate, Gen Zers are a little suspect of collaboration as they think you want something from them. Give them time to warm up to the idea of collaborating with others. One way is to invite them to initially collaborate via electronics which allows them to feel safe behind a screen as they learn to share their thoughts and new ideas to the group.

CLEAR OBJECTIVES IN THE WORKPLACE

Leaders who can clearly articulate the future of the organization and how each team member fits into that future increases the generational synchronicity within the workplace. Each generation will see the company differently in regard to vision and mission.

> *"If you had started doing anything two weeks ago, by today you would have been two weeks better at it."*
> —*John Mayer*

TRADITIONALISTS: Once this generation has trust in the company, they will believe what the leader says about the vision and mission of the company. Traditionalists are comfortable with following the path laid out by the leader.

BABY BOOMERS: This generation is willing to trust the company until you prove them wrong. They want to know where the leadership is taking the company and will follow as long as they feel secure that their position is still valuable.

GENERATION X: Gen Xers don't always trust an organization and will look for the leaders to work hard to earn their trust. Even when they know that the company is being honest with them, Gen Xers often doubt the company's authenticity and want to be reassured.

MILLENNIALS: A leader can tell a millennial whatever they want to; however, don't be surprised if they have already googled information about the vision and mission of an organization. If what a leader says lines up with that knowledge, the millennial will trust the company.

GENERATION Z: An organization's track record is what's most important to Gen Zers. They want to know how stable your company is and if your product will be around in twenty years. If a Gen Zer perceives long-term success for the company, they will stay connected.

RAISING UP LEADERS IN THE WORKPLACE (DEVELOPMENT)

As you think about raising up leaders from multiple generations and giving them the opportunity to develop, how does each generation see promotions and performance plans?

TRADITIONALISTS: The traditionalists who are still working are usually at the top of their game. They just want to be appreciated and given an opportunity to prove that what they know and do still adds value to the company.

BABY BOOMERS: Baby Boomers are not necessarily finished developing just because they are nearing retirement. They still want opportunities to develop new skills to contribute to the company in new ways. Boomers are usually good at being honest with their performance plans.

GENERATION X: Gen Xers want to develop and will do the hard work once they are convinced the company is going to be loyal to them. If there is any hint of disloyalty from a company, the Gen Xer will look elsewhere to be raised up. Gen Xers will also leave an organization for a promotion and later return to that same organization to accept another promotion, leap-frogging those who stayed and were loyal to the company.

MILLENNIALS: Millennials want to be challenged and raised up. They want a clear path for growth and development and will stay with an organization that invests in them. They will move on if they are not given opportunities to achieve their goals.

GENERATION Z: The young people from this generation are just entering the workforce in entry level positions but are looking to be raised up and developed. Finding even small ways to invest in them goes a long way toward their retention in your company.

EMPLOYEE EMPOWERMENT IN THE WORKPLACE

When a company learns how to empower its employees in ways that prepare them for what is next in their personal and professional development, it gives employees a sense of identity and ownership that can provide greater job satisfaction.

TRADITIONALISTS: Employees from this generation expect to be empowered because for them empowerment equals respect. They want to know that you trust in their capabilities enough to allow them to do the job.

BABY BOOMERS: To a baby boomer, empowerment is about position. When this employee has worked hard and has earned a new position or is promoted, they feel empowered to do the job because they were chosen for that position.

GENERATION X: Gen Xers view employee empowerment as the means for a company to demonstrate confidence in its employees. These understanding leads to a deeper respect for the organization and builds trust in the minds of Gen Xers which helps them fully engage in their jobs.

MILLENNIALS: For a millennial, failing to empower employees in not an option. This generation sees empowerment as a given because it's one of the best tools to generate great ideas for the company. They want to know they are a valuable part of the organization through a well-defined path for growth and development.

GENERATION Z: Empowerment is important to Gen Zers as they are looking for an organization that believes in itself enough to invest in its employees. This generation sees employee empowerment as a main source for growth and development as an organization.

By getting to the CORE your organization has the potential to foster a culture of leadership. It will give you the opportunity to see employees de-

veloped and given the chance to be all they can be. When you chose to invest in people, the future is bright. Employees who believe the organiza-

> *"Unless commitment is made, there are only promises and hopes; but no plans."*
> —Peter Drucker

tion has their best interest in mind will collaborate in the workplace, engage with the objectives of the organization, find ways to raise up others around them, and be empowered to bring about true and lasting change within your organization. These are the employees that have the potential to transform your organization and to help you build a legacy.

CONCLUSION: ARE YOU A LEGACY MAKER?

"Please think about your legacy because you are writing it every day."
—*Gary Vaynerchuk*

Are you willing to be a legacy maker? Legacy makers are supervisors, front-line employees, and CEOs. They are entrepreneurs. They are men and women who all have one thing in common: a desire to empower, promote, and launch their employees and to create an environment where leaders are developed and are prospering.

If we want to be remembered for something that lasts, we can't just coast through this life hoping that along the way we will make something to leave behind. Legacy makers realize that it's about standing up and moving forward. They understand that to leave a legacy it takes hard work, determination, and being intentional with how they interact with others.

A true legacy maker is concerned about changing culture at a grassroots level where people buy into an organization. Any organization that wishes to see lasting change must understand that culture change takes diligence and requires someone to lead the way. Legacy makers are leaders who are willing to be the first one through the wall and the first to acknowledge that the organization must think differently or suffer the consequences of outdated thinking. Legacy makers are not intimidated to take seriously the changes needed at all levels of the organization.

> A true legacy maker is concerned about CHANGING CULTURE at a grassroots level where people buy into an organization.

When I am consulting leaders who want to see change, I will often ask how far they are willing to go to see that change take place. I ask them how much they are willing to give up. How a leader answers these questions says a great deal about their level of readiness to truly commit to leaving behind a legacy. A leader who is truly committed to seeing change within their organization has the mark of becoming a legacy maker. A legacy maker must have the courage to let go of ego and status quo and move toward something bigger. Committing to this process it not easy; however, those who do are thinking like a legacy maker.

Legacy makers also commit to developing people and to fighting for the men and women who are part of their organizations. It's about envisioning a culture where people are encouraged to try something new and live outside the box. It's about being part of an organization where people are free to dream and are encouraged to be themselves. To empower people to function in their sweet spots is rare in this day and age, yet it is something that men and women from all generations appreciate.

Remember Mike, the CEO of Pure Energy? Mike chose not to retire following his 65th birthday. Instead, he decided to take the next four years to plan his exit strategy. Over those four years, Mike began the process of turning over Pure Energy to Susan who started her career at Pure Energy as a project manager. She was identified early on as having solid leadership potential. Mike worked with Susan to pinpoint areas of growth and helped her to lay out a path for professional development. Susan was part of the collaborative process for many years, being promoted to mid-level management which gave her the opportunity to lead an initiative to clarify several of the company's organizational objectives. Because of her firm leadership on this initiative, she was raised up and given the chief role on other projects. Due to her leadership skills, Mike empowered Susan to take the lead on a large company merger which she knocked out of the park.

Now at age 69 and ready to retire, Mike already knows that Susan is the next person for the position of CEO of Pure Energy. He shares with her his plans for retirement and they put together a succession plan. A few weeks later at his retirement party, Mike is able to share with the other employ-

> *"I'll bet most of the companies that are in life-or-death battles got into that kind of trouble because they didn't pay enough attention to developing their leaders."*
> —*Wayne Calloway*

ees all that Susan has accomplished and how he has complete confidence in her ability to take Pure Energy to the next level.

Mike understands that the legacy he is leaving behind consists of the people now gathered around him in the room. He looks around and sees all the generations together. He can genuinely say his organization truly operates with generational synchronicity. Mike stands to address his friends and work colleagues and scans the room for a moment, allowing the silence to speak loudly before beginning to talk. As he makes eye contact with each person in the room, he feels the moment sink in. Slowly the tears well up within his eyes as he reminisces about his time at Pure Energy and the lessons he has learned along the way.

> *"We believe that when the right talent meets the right opportunity in a company with the right philosophy, amazing transformation can happen."*
> —*Reid Hoffman*

Although his stories of the past years are meaningful and full of great memories, the legacy Mike is most proud of is the CORE leadership program that he put in place to enhance the culture of leadership within Pure Energy. As he steps away from the mic, he is certain that his company is in good hands and will long outlive him. This is a legacy he can be proud to leave behind.

ACKNOWLEDGMENTS

My intention for this book is to help both individuals and organizations navigate the changing workplace. I could not have done this without the support of my beautiful wife, Stephanie. You are the best part of me, and you make me a better person through my interactions with you. I love you! To my son Jordan, as a millennial cusper you challenged me to write from the heart about your generation with clarity and care. To my son Taylor, you along with your friends became my research subjects for Generation Z. Thanks for participating in this research – even when at times you didn't know it was happening.

I could never have accomplished this monumental endeavor without my editor, friend and sister-in-law, Michelle Baumgartner. You worked tirelessly to make this project a reality. I owe you so much more than words can express. You are a brilliant editor and through your words you made me sound so much better than I ever could myself. Thank you for all of your help and guidance as we wrote and rewrote so many sections.

To Ron Price, thank you for your friendship and guidance on this project.

You have given me direction as I look toward the future. Finally, thanks to my friend Gabrielle Bosché for the research you have done to move this conversation forward.

REFERENCES

1. "About Gore." *Gore Technologies*. http://www.gore.com/en_xx/aboutus/index. html (accessed December 2, 2011).

2. Cooper, Michael. "Census Officials, Citing Increasing Diversity, Say U.S. Will Be a 'Plurality Nation.'" *The New York Times*. https://www.nytimes. com/2012/12/13/us/us-will-have-no-ethnic-majority-census-finds.html (accessed December 20, 2015).

3. DeBord, Matthew. "A New Generation Gets a Name: 'Plurals.'" Southern California Public Radio. http://www.scpr.org/blogs/ economy/2012/04/30/5859/new-generation-gets-name-plurals/ (accessed June 10, 2014).

4. "Generations: Demographic Trends in Population and Workforce." *Catalyst*, July 20, 2017. http://www.catalyst.org/knowledge/generations-demographic-trends-population-and-workforce (accessed January 5, 2018).

5. Hans Finzel. *Empowered Leaders*. Nashville, TN: Thomas Nelson Publishers, 1998.

6. Hartman, Robert S. "Axiology as a Science," *The Journal of Human Relations, vol. 21*, no. 1, 1973. Updated: https://www.hartmaninstitute.org/ axiologyasascience/ (accessed December 2, 2011).

6. Henig, Robin Marantz. "What Is It About 20-Somethings?" *The New York Times Magazine*. https://www.nytimes.com/2010/08/22/magazine/22Adulthood-t. html?pagewanted=all (accessed March 10, 2011).

7. Johnson, Andy. *Pushing Back Entropy: Moving Teams from Conflict to Health*. N.P.: Restoration Publishing, 2014.

8. Keagan, Robert and Lisa Laskow Lahey. *An Everyone Culture: Becoming a Deliberately Developmental Organization*. Cambridge, MA: Harvard Business Review Press, 2016.

9. Keller, Gary with Jay Papasan. *The ONE Thing: The Surprisingly Simple Truth behind Extraordinary Results*. Austin, TX: Rellek Publishing Partners, 2012.

10. Levin, Amelia. "Trend: Generation Z—Today's College Consumer." *Foodservice Equipment & Supplies Magazine*, July 3, 2017. http://www.fesmag.com/news/14844-trend-generation-z%E2%80%94today%E2%80%99s-college-consumer (accessed July 17, 2017).

11. Marquet, David. *Turn the Ship Around!: A True Story of Turning Followers into Leaders*. New York, NY: Portfolio Publishing, 2012.

12. "Mars Who We Are." *Mars, Incorporated*. http://www.mars.com/global/about-us (accessed December 2, 2011).

13. Mitchell, Whit. (October 17, 2011). Personal interview.

14. Palmer, Kimberly. "Boomers Boosting Economy." *AARP Magazine*, March 13, 2017. https://www.aarp.org/work/on-the-job/info-2017/older-workers-remain-on-job-fd.html (accessed December 29, 2017).

15. Pianin, Eric. "10,000 Boomers Turn 65 Every Day. Can Medicare and Social Security Handle It?" *The Fiscal Times*. http://www.thefiscaltimes.com/2017/05/09/10000-Boomers-Turn-65-Every-Day-Can-Medicare-and-Social-Security-Handle-It (accessed May 20, 2017).

16. Sanburn, Josh. "Here's what MTV Is Calling the Generation after Millennials." *Time Magazine*, updated: December 1, 2015. http://time.com/4130679/millennials-mtv-generation/ (accessed December 12, 2016).

17. "TTI Success Insights® Products." Target Training International, Ltd. https://www.ttisuccessinsights.com/products/ (accessed March 1, 2017). *TTI Success Insights® DISC is a registered trademark of Target Training International, Ltd. TTI 12 Driving Forces® (Motivators) is a registered trademark of Target Training International, Ltd. TTI Talent Insights® is a registered trademark of Target Training International, Ltd.*

Made in the USA
Columbia, SC
10 October 2023

23980869R00083